About the Publisher

## *The New York Institute of Finance*

***. . . more than just books.***

NYIF offers practical, applied education and training in a wide range of financial topics:

- *Classroom training:* evenings, mornings, noon hour
- *Seminars:* one- and two-day professional and introductory programs
- *Customized training:* need-specific, on your site or ours, in New York City, throughout the United States, anywhere in the world
- *Independent study:* self-paced learning—basic, intermediate, advanced
- *Exam preparation:* NASD licensing (including Series 7), CFA prep, state life and health insurance licensing

Subjects of books and training programs include the following:

- *Account Executive Training*
- *Brokerage Operations*
- *Futures Trading*
- *International Corporate Finance*
- *Options as a Strategic Investment*
- *Securities Transfer*
- *Technical Analysis*

*When Wall Street professionals think* **training,** *they think* **NYIF.**

# THE SECURITIES INDUSTRY GLOSSARY

Second Edition

New York Institute of Finance

**Library of Congress Cataloging-in-Publication Data**

The Securities industry glossary.

1. Securities--Dictionaries. I. New York Institute of Finance.
HG4513.S427 1988 332.63'2'0321 88-5205
ISBN 0-13-798778-1

This publication is designed to provide accurate and authoritative information in regard to the subject matter covered. It is sold with the understanding that the publisher is not engaged in rendering legal, accounting, or other professional service. If legal advice or other expert assistance is required, the services of a competent professional person should be sought.

*From a Declaration of Principles Jointly Adopted by a Committee of the American Bar Association and a Committee of Publishers and Associations*


A Division of Simon & Schuster, Inc.
70 Pine Street, New York, NY 10270-0003



Printed in the United States of America

10 9 8 7 6 5 4 3 2 1

New York Institute of Finance
(NYIF Corp.)
70 Pine Street
New York, New York 10270-0003

# Introduction

The language of securities is perhaps the most colorful of all the professions. What is a white knight? A red herring? How does a greenshoe differ from greenmail? How do you blue-sky an issue? What do you find on the pink sheets?

These and well over 2000 other securities related terms are defined in this book. These are the very terms used by securities professionals "on the street" and found every day in the financial news.

Both industry practitioners—entrant and veteran alike—and investors will benefit from having *The Securities Industry Glossary* on their desks. In it you will find the meanings of words having to do with:

* Stocks—common and preferred
* Bonds—corporates, municipals, governments
* Mortgage-backed securities
* Options
* Futures
* The over-the-counter market
* The exchanges
* Operations
* Compliance
* And much more.

### ABC Agreement

A contract by which an individual purchases a seat on an exchange through funds advanced by a partnership (or corporation). The agreement stipulates, among other things, whether the seat will be (a) retained by the individual and another bought for the company; (b) sold and the proceeds remitted to the firm; or (c) transferred to the firm for a nominal consideration should the individual leave the firm or die.

### Account Executive (AE)

A brokerage firm employee who advises clients and handles orders for them. The AE must be registered with the National Association of Securities Dealers (NASD) before taking orders from clients. Also known as registered representative (RR) or stockbroker.

### Accounting Spread

The annual net spread between assets and liabilities calculated using pro forma income results.

### Account Statement

A statement sent periodically (at least quarterly) to clients, showing the status of their accounts with a broker/dealer. Most broker/dealers send monthly accounts summarizing all transactions during the previous period, as well as an accounting of credits, debits, and long and short positions.

### Accounting Equation

A formula used in totalling balance sheets:

Total Assets = Total Liabilities + Shareholder's Equity.

The formula may be restated in terms of shareholder's equity or in terms of total liabilities as follows:

Total Assets – Total Liabilities = Shareholder's Equity or

Total Assets – Shareholder's Equity = Total Liabilities.

### Accounts Payable

A current liability showing the amounts due others within a period of one year when such liability resulted from the purchase or manufacturing of inventory.

### Accounts Receivable

Any money due a business for merchandise or securities that it has sold or for services it has rendered. This is a key determinant in analyzing a company's liquidity.

### Accretion

The accumulation of accrued coupon payments as added principal.

### Accrued Expenses

A liability, either current or long-term, showing the estimated amounts due others for services rendered or goods received.

### Accrued Interest

The amount of interest due the seller, from the buyer, upon settlement of a bond trade.

Prorated interest due since the last interest payment date.

### Accumulated Depletion (Depreciation)

*See* Allowance for Depletion.

### Accumulation Area

In technical analysis, a lateral move in the market price of a security, indicating that buyers are willing to purchase at the current price.

### Accumulation Unit

A share of a variable annuity fund, the value of which is calculated to be the value of the entire fund divided by the number of accumulation units. The term is generally used during the accumulation phase of the annuity.

*See* Annuity Unit.

### Acid Test Ratio

The value of cash, cash equivalents, and accounts receivable (the quick assets) divided by current liabilities. A measurement of corporate liquidity. Also known as quick asset ratio or liquidity ratio.

### Acting Jointly or in Concert

A term used by all the exchanges trading options in defining certain position and exercise limits. No person, or group of people "acting jointly or in concert," may exceed those limits set by regulation, in order to avoid any group controling a market.

### Activating Sale

*See* Electing Sale.

### Active Bonds (The "Free" Crowd)

A category of debt securities that the NYSE Floor Department expects to trade frequently and that are consequently handled "freely" in the trading ring in much the same manner as stocks.

*See* Inactive Bonds.

### Active Box

A physical location where securities are held awaiting action on them.

### Adjustable Rate Mortgage (ARM)

A mortgage agreement whose interest rate may be adjusted to keep pace with a fluctuating market. Also referred to as a Variable Rate Mortgage or Floating Rate Mortgage.

### Adjusted Debit Balance

The net money borrowed by a brokerage customer in a margin account as a result of both settled and unsettled transactions. It includes SMA.

### Adjustment Bonds

*See* Income (Adjustment) Bonds.

### ADR

*See* American Depository Receipt (ADR).

### Administrator

A court-appointed person or institution charged with the maintenance and distribution of the assets and liabilities of a deceased, used when the deceased did *not* leave a will.

*See* Executor/Executrix.

### Advance-Decline Theory

A market theory that uses the relative number of advances versus declines in relation to total issues traded to make buying and/or selling decisions. Formula = A – D/V.

### Advertising Practices

In accordance with Section 1 of the NASD Rules of Fair Practice, any communication designed for public consumption—including sales literature, market letters, and recruiting materials—must not contain false or misleading statements of any material facts. All such communications must be reasonable and accurate as well as initialed or signed by a registered principal of the advertising firm and filed for three years. It must also be reviewed by the NASD Executive Office in Washington, D.C. within five days after its initial usage.

### AE

*See* Account Executive.

### AE Credits

This is a soft dollar amount credited to an Account Executive in payment of his order. The trader determines the amount to be paid which is based on the amortized amount of the trade. The hard dollars received by the AE will be a percentage of that amount.

### Affiliated Members

Clearing corporations of other stock exchanges that have signed agreements with the Stock Clearing Corporation of the NYSE to be bound by the bylaws and rules of the exchange and to make payments and deliveries as prescribed.

### Affiliated Person

Anyone in a position to influence decisions made in a corporation, including officers, directors, principal stockholders, and members of their immediate families. Their shares are often referred to as "control stock."

### Aftermarket

A market for a security either over the counter or on an exchange after an initial public offering has been made.

*See* Free-Riding; Hot Issue; Stabilization; Withholding.

### Against the Box

*See* Short Against the Box.

### Aged Fail

An incomplete contract between two broker/dealers. A contract becomes "aged fail" if it remains unsettled after 30 days from the time that delivery and payment should have been completed.

### Agency Transaction

*See* As Agent.

### Agent

*See* As Agent.

### Agreement Among Underwriters

An agreement among members of an underwriting syndicate specifying the syndicate manager, his duties, and his privileges, among other things.

*See* Underwriter's Retention; Underwriting Agreement.

### All Equity

Interim finanacing in which the money is provided entirely by the owners. Sometimes the purpose is to refinance or sell the project when its economic value as a going operation has been established.

### Allied Member

Broker-partnership: a general partner who does not own a seat on the stock exchange.

Broker-corporation: a voting stockholder employee of the firm who does not own a seat on the stock exchange and either (a) owns 5 percent or more of its voting stock, (b) serves as director on its board, or (c) has been designated as a principal executive officer by the firm.

*See* Allied Members.

### Allied Members

Either (1) all general partners who are not members of the exchange; or (2) voting stockholder employees of a member corporation who (a) own 5 percent or more of the voting stock; (b) are directors of the board; or (c) have been designated by the corporation as principal executive officers. Allied members must pass a written examination and be bound by the NYSE Constitution and Rules.

*See* Allied Member.

### Allocations

The process of specifying pools to satisfy the demands of TBA contracts in such a way as to maximize the spread between the purchase price and sales price of the pools.

### All-or-None (AON) Offering

A "best-efforts" offering of newly issued securities in which the corporation instructs the investment banker to cancel the entire offering (sold and unsold) if all of it cannot be distributed.

### All-or-None Order

An order to buy or sell more than one round lot of stock at one time and at a designated price or better. It must not be executed until both conditions can be satisfied simultaneously.

### Allowance for Depletion

(Also called Accumulated Depletion.) The portion of the cost of acquiring and putting into production a natural asset (e.g., oil wells, gold mines) that has been written off against income (expensed). A balance sheet account showing the amount of the cost of a natural wasting asset that has been charged against income. For example:

| | |
|---|---:|
| Gold mine, at cost | $100,000 |
| Less: Allowance for Depletion | 25,000 |
| Net Book Value | $ 75,000 |

### Allowance for Depreciation

(Also called Accumulated Depreciation.) That portion of the cost of acquiring and putting into production buildings and equipment that have been written off against income (expensed). A balance sheet account showing the amount of an asset's cost that has been charged against income since its acquisition. For example:

| | |
|---|---:|
| Machinery, at cost | $10,000 |
| Less: Allowance for Depreciation | 3,000 |
| Net Book Value | $ 7,000 |

### Alpha

*See* Differential Return.

### Alternative (Either/Or) Order

An order to do either of two alternatives such as either buy at a limit or buy stop for the same security. Execution of one part of the order automatically cancels the other.

*See* One Cancels the Other.

### American Depository Receipt (ADR)

A receipt showing evidence that shares of a foreign corporation are held on deposit or are under the control of a U.S. banking institution. Used to facilitate transactions and expedite transfer of beneficial ownership for a foreign security in the United States.

### American Stock Exchange Clearing Corporation

A wholly owned subsidiary of the American Stock Exchange charged with the responsibility of assisting member firms to settle trades. The corporation has contracted with the Securities Industry Automation Corporation to perform all its duties except the rule-making function.

### American Stock Market Value Index

A market index for all common stocks listed on the ASE, prepared daily and grouped by geographic locale and industrial category.

### American Stock Exchange Price Change Index

An "unweighted" market index for all common stocks listed on the ASE, prepared hourly.

### AMEX

An acronym for American Stock Exchange, Inc.

### AMEX Rule 411

The American Stock Exchange's version of the "know your customer" rule of the NYSE.

*See* Rule 405.

### AMFOD

An acronym for Association of Member Firm Option Departments, a division of the SIA dedicated to improving the option market.

### Amortization

A generic term including depreciation, depletion, and write-offs of intangibles, prepaid expenses, and deferred charges.

### Amortized Amount

The outstanding principal or loan amount of the mortgages in a pool. To obtain the amount, multiply the original face value by the current factor value as announced by the issuer, GNMA or other agencies of the government.

### "And Interest"

A bond transaction in which the buyer pays the seller a contract price plus interest accrued since the corporation's last interest payment.

### Annual Audit

SEC Rule 17a-5 requires that every broker/dealer be audited at least annually by a firm of Certified Public Accountants.

### Annual Report

A formal statement issued yearly by a corporation to its shareowners. It shows assets, liabilities, equity, revenues, expenses, and so forth. It is a reflection of the corporation's condition at the close of the business year, and the results of operations for that year.

### Annuity

A contract between an insurance company and an individual whereby the insurance company agrees to make periodic payment to the individual, for a certain period or for the life of the individual.

### Annuity Unit

A term used to describe accumulation units of a variable annuity once distribution has begun.

### Annunciator Board

A paging system on the New York Stock Exchange by which telephone clerks summon brokers using numbers with colored markers attached.

### AON Offering

*See* All-or-Non (AON) Offering.

### AON Order

*See* All-or-None (AON) Order.

### Approved Person

A person who has control of but who is not an employee of a member firm. An approved person must agree to be bound by the constitution and the rules of the exchange. He/she must also be approved by the board of governors of the exchange. A good example of an approved person is a member of the board of directors of a member corporation who is not an employee of that corporation.

### Arbitrage

The simultaneous purchase and sale of the same or equal securities in such a way as to take advantage of price differences prevailing in separate markets, with relatively low risk. In equities, the profit is "net price"; in fixed income trading, it is "net interest rate spread."

*See* Bona Fide Arbitrage; Risk Arbitrage.

### Arbitrage Bonds

All bonds found in violation of federal arbitrage regulations as deemed by the Internal Revenue Service. If the IRS deems a bond an arbitrage bond, then the interest becomes taxable and must therefore be included in each bondholder's gross income for federal tax purposes. Refer to IRS Regs. 1.103-13 through 1.103-15.

### Arbitrageur

One who engages in arbitrage.

### Arrearage

Undeclared and/or unpaid dividends due holders of cumulative preferred stock.

### ARM

*See* Adjustable Rate Mortgage.

### As Agent

The role of a broker/dealer firm when it acts as an intermediary, or broker, between its customer and another customer, a market maker, or a contrabroker. For this service the firm receives a stated commission or fee. This is an "agency transaction."

*See* As Principal.

### As Principal

The role of a broker/dealer firm when it buys and sells for its own account. In a typical transaction, it buys from a market maker or contrabroker and sells to a customer at a fair and reasonable markup; if it buys from a customer and sells to the market maker at a higher price, the trade is called a mark-down.

*See* As Agent.

### Ascending Tops

In technical analysis, a chart pattern of a security's price in which each peak is higher than the one preceding. The upward movement usually means that the upward trend is likely to continue and would therefore be considered bullish.

### Ascending Triangle

A chart pattern in technical analysis in which the lows move progressively higher, while the highs encounter resistance at one price level.

### Ask-Bid System

A system used to place a market order. A market order is one the investor wants executed immediately at the best prevailing price. The market order to buy requires a purchase at the lowest offering (asked) price, and a market order to sell requires a sale at the highest (bid) price. The bid price is what the dealer is willing to pay for the stock, while the ask price is the price at which the dealer will sell to individual investors. The difference between the bid and ask prices is the spread.

*See* Bid-and-Quotations.

### Asset Management

Investment strategy involving the capability for originating loans or investments, evaluating collateral value, and the borrower's ability to repay, as well as the servicing of loans.

### Asset Management Account

An account at a bank, savings and loan institution, or brokerage house that can combine banking services like checking accounts, credit cards, and debit cards with brokerage features, such as buying and selling securities on margin. One monthly statement combines all financial transactions.

### Assets

Everything of value that a company owns or has due: cash, buildings, and machinery (fixed assets); and patents and good will (intangible assets).

*See* Equity; Liabilities.

### Assign

*See* Early Exercise; Exercise.

### Assignment Form (Notice)

A form used for the transfer of ownership by a registered security owner. Usually, on the reverse side of a registered security certificate is a form where the registered owner may assign new ownership, but a separate piece of paper may also be used.

Form used by the Options Clearing Corporation to notify a member firm that an option has been exercised against a client who wrote a security option.

### Assignment of Mortgage

An assignment—or notice of transfer or equivalent instrument—that reflects the sale of the mortgage property to certificated holders. This assignment may be in blanket form where permitted by law.

### Associate Members of Stock Clearing Corporation

Organizations whose clearance operations are handled by the Stock Clearing Corporation but who do not belong to the NYSE.

### Associated Person

As defined by the SEC, a partner, officer, director, salesperson, trader, manager, or any employee of a broker/dealer organization.

### Associate Specialists

Assistants to regular specialists who do not solicit orders or stabilize markets as principals. They may act as agents but only in the presence and under the supervision of a regular or relief specialist.

### Association of Member Firm Option Departments (AMFOD)

A division of the Securities Industry Association dedicated to improving the option market.

### At-the-Close Order

An order to be executed, at the market, at the close, or as near as practicable to the close of trading for the day.

### At-the-Market

A price representing what a buyer would pay and what a seller would take in an arm's-length transaction assuming normal competitive forces;

an order to buy or sell immediately at the currently available price.

*See* Market Order.

### At-the-Money

A term used to describe a security option where the strike price and market price are the same.

### At-the-Opening (Opening Only) Order

An order to buy or sell at a limited price on the initial transaction of the day for a given security; if unsuccessful, it is automatically cancelled.

### Auction Marketplace

A term used to describe an organized exchange where transactions are held in the open and any exchange member present may join in.

### Autex System

System that uses electronic screens to allow broker/dealers and other subscribers to communicate about blocks of stock. Any transactions can then be executed on a securities exchange or in the over-the-counter market.

### Authorized Stock

The maximum number of shares that the state secretary permits a corporation to issue.

### Automatic Exercise

To protect the holder of an expiring in-the-money option, the Options Clearing Corporation automatically exercises the option for the holder. Only the owner can instruct to do otherwise.

### Automatic Reinvestment of Distributions

A feature of voluntary and contractual accumulation mutual fund plans by which dividends and/or capital gains are automatically reinvested in additional shares or in fractions of a share.

### Automatic Withdrawal

A privilege of participants in a voluntary accumulation or completed contractual mutual fund plan by which the custodial bank disburses to the planholder a specified sum of money each month or quarter. If mutual fund distributions are insufficient to meet this demand for money, an appropriate number of shares will be redeemed.

### Average

A stock market indicator based on the sum of market values for a selected sample of stocks, divided either by the number of issues or by a divisor that allows for stock splits or other changes in capitalization. The most widely used average is issued by Dow-Jones.

### Average Down

The practice of purchasing additional shares of the same issue as its market price declines so that the investor's cost per share for his entire holding will also decline.

### Average Up

The practice of purchasing additional shares of the same issue as its market price rises so that the investor's cost per share for his entire holding will also rise.

### Average Life

In mortgage-backed securities, the weighted average time to principal repayment. It is used as an approximate single maturity, where the mean or average maturity is used to describe the life of the instrument.

*See* Duration and Half-Life.

For whole loans, average life is calculated to produce a single value to measure the time-weighting of principal repayments. Average life reflects the average time the original investment dollars are outstanding; it is not a measure of price volatility.

### Averaging the Dollar

Incorrect term used for dollar cost averaging.

*See* Dollar Cost Averaging.

### Away from Me

When a market maker does not initiate a quotation, transaction, or market in an issue, he says it is "away from me."

### Away from the Market

An order where the limit bid is below (or the limit offer is above) the quote for the security. For example, if a quote for a security is 20 to 20½, a limit order to buy at 19 is "away from the market."

### B

A symbol on the ticker tape that means a quote report rather than a trade report.

### Baby Bond

A bond with a face value of less than $1,000, usually in $100 denominations.

### Backdating

The predating of a letter of intent (by as much as 90 days) to allow an investor to incorporate recent large deposits for the purpose of qualifying for a load discount on a purchase of open-end investment company shares.

### Backing Away

The practice of an OTC market maker who refuses to honor his or her quoted bid-and-asked prices for at least 100 shares, or 10 bonds, as the case may be. This action is outlawed under the NASD Rules of Fair Practice.

### Back Month

A remote deferred month in futures contract trading.

### Back Office

An industry expression used to describe non-sales departments of a brokerage concern, particularly a firm's P&S and cashier departments.

### Backspread

*See* Reverse Strategy.

### Back to Back

Selling a security immediately prior to its purchase so that the transaction carries no market risk for the seller.

### Back Up

A reverse in a stock market trend.

### Balanced Companies (Funds)

Investment companies that strive to minimize market risks while at the same time earning reasonable current income with varying percentages of bonds and preferred and common stocks.

### Balance Orders

The pairing off of each issue traded in the course of a day by the same member to arrive at a net balance of securities to receive or deliver. The net difference between buyers and sellers on the opening of the market allows the specialist to appropriately open the market.

### Balance Sheet

A condensed statement showing the nature and amount of a company's assets, liabilities, and capital on a given date. It shows in dollar amounts what the company owns, what it owes, and the ownership interest (shareholders' equity).

### Balance Sheet Equation

*See* Accounting Equation.

### Balloon Effect

A term used to describe a serial bond issue having lower principal repayments in the early years of its life and higher principal repayments in the later years.

### Ban

*See* Bond Anticipation Note.

### Bank Dealer

A bank engaged in buying and selling government securities, municipal securities, or certain money market instruments.

### Bankers' Acceptances

Bills of exchange guaranteed (accepted) by a bank or trust company for payment within one to six months. Used to provide manufacturers and exporters with capital to operate between the time of manufacturing (or exporting) and payment by purchasers. Bids and offers in the secondary marketplace are at prices discounted from the face value.

### Bank Float

The financial advantage realized by banks as a result of the normal delay in transferring funds between banks in processing transactions.

### Bank for International Settlements (BIS)

An organization of central banks and other financial institutions that: (1) acts as a forum for discussion of international monetary issues, and (2) acts as a clearing bank—that is, holds deposits, keeps gold reserves, and handles central bank deposits/withdrawals.

### Bank Holding Company

A company established so that a bank may engage in such nonbank activities as leasing, mortgage banking, or consumer credit.

### Banking and Securities Industry Committee (BASIC)

A financial industry group formed to promote standardization in option and certificate processing systems.

### Bank Instructions

*See* Delivery Instructions.

### Bankruptcy Proof Entity

A legal entity whose asset/liability structure is such that, under all realistic scenarios, proceeds from sale or utilization of assets are great enough to meet all liabilities.

### Banks for Cooperatives (Co-Op)

An agency under the supervision of the Farm Credit Administration that makes and services loans for farmers' cooperative financing. The agency is capitalized by the issuance of bonds whose interest is free from state and local income taxes.

### Bar Chart

In technical analysis, a chart used to plot stock movements with darkened vertical bars indicating all prices. Most charts are issued daily, weekly, or monthly.

### Barron's Confidence Index

A market index that measures investors' willingness to take risks according to yields on rated bonds.

### Base Market Value

In the construction of a market index, the average value of securities traded at a certain time. All movement is usually reported in terms of a dollar or percentage change from an original value, or "base."

### BASIC

*See* Banking and Securities Industry Committee.

### Basis Point

One one-hundredth of a percentage point. For example, if a Treasury bill yielding 7.17% changes in price so that it now yields 7.10%, it is said to have declined seven basis points.

### Basis Price Odd-Lot Order

An odd-lot order executed on a fictitious round-lot price somewhere between the prevailing bid and offering, if (1) the issue doesn't trade throughout the day; (2) the spread is at least two full points; and (3) the customer requests such an execution.

### Bearer Bond

A bond that does not have the owner's name registered on the books of the issuing corporation and that is payable to the bearer.

### Bearer Form

Securities issued in such a form as not to allow for the owner's name to be imprinted on the security. The bearer of the security is presumed to be the owner who collects interest by clipping and depositing coupons semiannually.

### Bearish

An adjective used to describe an opinion or outlook where one anticipates decline in price of the general market, of an underlying stock, or of both.

*See* Bullish.

### Bear Market

A securities market characterized by declining prices.

*See* Bull Market.

### Bear Raiders

Groups of speculators who pool capital and sell short to drive prices down and who then buy to cover their short positions—thereby pocketing large profits. This practice was outlawed by the Securities Exchange Act of 1934.

*See* Raiders.

### Bear Spread

An option spread so designed that a profit will result if the underlying security declines in the market. The trader buys (long) the higher strike price and sells (writes) the lower strike price.

### Beneficial Owner

The owner of securities who receives all the benefits, even though they are registered in the "street name" of a brokerage firm or nominee name of a bank handling his or her account.

### Best-Efforts Offering

An offering of newly issued securities in which the investment banker acts merely as an agent of the corporation, promising only his "best efforts" in making the issue a success but not guaranteeing the corporation its money for any unsold portion.

*See* All-or-None (AON) Offering.

### Beta

A measurement that quantifies the correlation between the movement of a stock and the movement of the stock market as a whole. Not to be mistaken with volatility.

*See* Volatility.

### Bid-and-Asked Quotation (or Quote)

The bid is the highest price anyone has declared that he/she wants to pay for a security at a given time; the asked is the lowest price anyone will accept at the same time.

*See* Offer.

### Bidding Limitations

Any restriction in a notice of sale on the terms of bids submitted by prospective underwriters. Such restrictions could include the number of different interest rates permitted, the maximum range of interest, and whether a bid is allowable.

### Bidding Syndicate

Two or more underwriters working together to submit a proposal to underwrite a new issue of municipal securities.

*See* Syndicate.

### Big Bang

The term applied to October 27, 1986, when London equity and government debt markets were freed of fixed commission requirements.

### Big Board

A popular slang term for the New York Stock Exchange.

### Big Four

The nickname for Japan's major brokerages: Nomura Securities Ltd., Nikko Securities Ltd., Daiwa Securities Ltd., and Yamaichi Securities Ltd.

### BIS

*See* Bank for International Settlements.

### Black-Scholes Model

A formula used to calculate theoretical option prices from stock price, strike price, volatility, and time to expiration. A by-product of the model is the exact calculation of the delta.

*See* Delta.

### Blanket Certification Form (NASD Form FR-1)

A form required of all foreign broker/dealers or banks that are not participating in a hot issue distribution as underwriters. It is submitted once, the first time such participation is agreed upon, and indicates that the participants understand the regulations governing hot issues and will abide by them.

### Blanket (Fidelity) Bond Insurance

Blanket insurance covering all employees, officers, and partners of NYSE member organizations that protects investors against misplacement, fraudulent trading, and check forgery. Such coverage is required by the NYSE Constitution.

### Blind Pool

A limited partnership, typically for investment in real estate, in which the general partner does not specify the properties intended for acquisition. Investors can evaluate the investment only in terms of the general partner's track record. They cannot look at prices paid and rental income to evaluate the partnership's potential.

### Block

A large amount of securities, generally a minimum of either 10,000 shares or $200,000.

### Block Positioner

A broker/dealer who takes positions for his or her own account and risk in order to facilitate a large purchase or sale of securities by customers that would otherwise be disruptive to the market. A block positioner may be given relief under Regulation T to assist the financing of such positions.

### Blowout

A securities offering that sells out almost immediately.

### Blue Chip Stocks

Common stocks of well known companies with histories of profit growth and dividend payment, as well as quality management, products, and services. Blue chip stocks are usually high-priced and low-yielding. The term "blue chip" comes from the game of poker in which the blue chip holds the highest value.

### Blue List

A publication of Standard & Poor's Corporation advertising municipal bonds available in the secondary market.

### Blue Room

One of the small trading areas just off the main trading floor of the New York Stock Exchange.

### Blue-Sky Laws

State securities laws pertaining to registration requirements and procedures for issuers, broker/dealers, their employees, and other associated persons of those entities.

### Blue-Skying the Issue

The efforts of the underwriters' lawyers to analyze and investigate state laws regulating the distribution of securities and to qualify particular issues under these laws.

### Board Broker

A member of an options exchange appointed by that exchange to handle public limit orders left in his/her care by floor brokers. In performing this function, he/she is said to be running the "public book." These brokers' prime responsibility is to ensure that a fair, orderly, and competitive market exists in the classes of options to which they are assigned.

*See* Market Maker; Specialist.

### Board of Arbitration

A three-to-five-member NASD board, appointed ad hoc by the Board of Governors, to arbitrate disputes involving transactions among members, nonmembers, and customers.

*See* Code of Arbitration.

A board appointed by the chairman of the NYSE Board of Directors, comprised of members and allied members who serve in various ways and numbers to settle disputes arising among members or between members, allied members, and nonmembers.

### Board of Directors

A 20-man board that governs the NYSE, elected by the general membership for two years. These directors, in turn, elect a chairperson for a variable term of office, and the chairperson also participates in policy decisions.

### Board of Governors

The governing body of the NASD, most of whom are elected by the general membership; the remainder are elected by the board itself.

*See* Federal Reserve Board.

### Boiler Room Sales

The use of high-pressure sales tactics to promote purchases and sales of securities.

### Bona Fide Arbitrage

Arbitrage transactions by professional traders that take profitable advantage of prices for the same or convertible securities in different markets. The risk is usually minimal and the profit correspondingly small.

*See* Risk Arbitrage; Special Arbitrage Account.

### Bond

A certificate representing creditorship in a corporation and issued by the corporation to raise capital. The company pays interest on a bond issue at specified dates and eventually redeems it at maturity, paying principal plus interest due.

*See* Bearer Bond; Collateral Trust Bond; Equipment Trust Bond; Income Bond; Mortgage Bond; Receiver's Certificate; Registered Bond; Serial Bond; Tax-Exempt Securities; United States Government Securities.

### Bond Amortization Fund

An account in a sinking fund. The issuer makes periodic deposits of money eventually to be used to purchase bonds on the open market or to pay the cost of calling bonds.

### Bond and Preferred Stock Companies

Investment companies that emphasize stability of income. In the case of the municipal bond companies, income exempt from federal taxation is the chief goal.

### Bond Anticipation Note (BAN)

A short-term municipal debt instrument usually offered on a discount basis. The proceeds of a forthcoming bond issue are pledged to pay the note at maturity.

### Bond Broker

A member of the NYSE or any other exchange who executes orders in the bond room as a continuing practice.

### Bond Buyer

A book, published monthly, that lists all pools issued in the market and their current month's factors.

### Bonded Debt

The portion of an issuer's total indebtedness represented by outstanding bonds of various types.

### Bond Fund

An investment company with a diversified portfolio of municipal securities. Units or shares in the investment company are sold to investors. Unit investment trusts (UIT) and managed funds are the two basic types of bond funds.

### Bond Interest Distribution

Bonds that are traded at a market price "and interest" require an adjustment for the interest on the settlement date. The buyer therefore pays the seller the price plus interest accrued since the last payment date, and the buyer is thereby entitled to the next full payment of interest. The interest due is calculated by multiplying Principal × Rate × Time.

*See* Ex-Dividend Date.

### Bond Issue

Bonds (1) sold in one or more series; (2) authorized under the same indenture or resolution; and (3) having the same date.

### Bond Ordinance (Resolution)

A document (or documents) authorizing the issuance and sale of municipal securities. The issuance of securities is usually approved in the authorizing resolution, while the sale is typically authorized on a separate document called the "sale" or "award" resolution. When all such resolutions are read together, they become the bond resolution describing the nature of the obligation and the issuer's duties to the bondholders.

### Bond Power

*See* Stock (or Bond) Power.

### Bond Purchase Agreement

The contract between the issuer and underwriter that sets down the final terms, conditions, and prices by which the underwriter purchases an issue of municipal securities.

### Bond Ratio

The relationship of all bonds outstanding to the total capitalization of a corporation.

### Bond Record/Stock Record

A brokerage firm record showing the beneficial owner (long) and the location (short) of every security.

### Bond Room

Formerly, the room at the New York Stock Exchange where bonds are traded.

### Bond Value

The dollar amount of bonds that a mortgage's scheduled cash flow will support, with the amount limited to the unpaid mortgage balance.

### Book Value

The net tangible asset value per share of common stock. It is total assets less intangibles, minus total liabilities, minus the redemption value of preferred stock outstanding, divided by the common shares outstanding.

### Borrower

The individuals or entity obligated to repay the debt secured by the mortgage property. Any individual who meets the financial requirements of Freddie Mac must sign the note. For a home mortgage, the borrower must be an individual or individuals.

### Borrowing Power of Securities

The money invested in securities on margin, shown in the customer's monthly statement. The margin limit is usually 50 percent of their stock values, 30 percent of their bond values, and full value of their cash equivalent assets.

The securities pledged to a lender as collateral for a loan.

### BOT

Industry abbreviation for "bought."

*See* SLO.

Abbreviation for balance of trade.

Abbreviation for board of trustees (mutual savings bank industry).

### Bought Deal

A commitment by a group of underwriters to guarantee performance by buying the securities from the issuer themselves, usually entailing some financial risk for the underwriters (or syndicate).

### Box

A section of a cashier department where securities are stored temporarily. The department's responsibilities are sometimes subdivided to monitor both an active box and a free box for securities held by the firm.

### Box Spread

An option arbitrage. A bull spread and a bear spread are combined to create a profit with no risk.

### Branch Office Manager (BOM)

The person charged with one or more of a member firm's branch offices. This person must meet certain requirements, such as passing a special exchange examination. Those who supervise the sales activities of three or more account executives must also pass the branch office manager examination.

### Branch Wire

An order or message from the branch office that is carried to another branch or to the home office through a dedicated telecommunications network.

### Breadth Index

The net securities advanced or declined for a given day's trading divided by the total issues traded. For example:

| | |
|---|---|
| Advances | 500 |
| Declines | 600 |
| Unchanged | 200 |
| | 1,300 |

$$\frac{600-500}{1{,}300} = 7.69\%$$

### Break

A term used for any out-of-balance condition. A money break means that debits and credits are not equal. A trade break means that some information, such as that from a contrabroker, is missing to complete the trade.

### Breakeven Point

The stock price (or prices) at which a particular strategy of transaction neither makes nor loses money. In options, the result at the expiration date in the strategy. A "dynamic" breakeven point changes as time passes.

### Breakeven Prepayment Rate

The prepayment rate producing a required cash flow on a pass-through security.

A cash flow yield that meets the required spread over Treasuries of a specified average life or duration.

### Breakeven Yield

The point during a given period at which a strategy produces the same (no more, no less) yield as in a previous time period.

### Breakout

In technical analysis, the rise through a resistance level or the decline through a support level by the market price of a security.

### Breakpoint

The dollar level of investment necessary to qualify a purchaser for a discounted sales charge on a quantity purchase of shares of an open-end management company.

*See* Backdating; Letter of Intent.

### Breakpoint Sales

The soliciting of mutual fund orders in dollar amounts just below the breakpoint level (within $1,000). This practice is considered contrary to equitable principles of trade.

### Broker

An agent, often a member of a stock exchange firm or the head of a member firm, who handles the public's orders to buy and sell securities and commodities, for which service a commission is charged. The definition does not include a bank.

*See* As Agent; As Principal.

### Broker's Broker

Also known as a municipal securities broker's broker, a person who deals only with other municipal securities brokers and dealers, not with the general public.

### Broker's Collateral (Call) Loan

A broker's loan from a commercial bank using margin account customers' securities or firm-owned securities as the bank's protection. It is sometimes referred to as a call loan because either party can terminate it on twenty-four-hour notice.

*See* Call Money Rate.

### Bucket Shop

An organization that accepts customer orders but does not immediately execute them. It waits until, and if, the market acts contrary to the customer's expectations, then executes the order but confirms it to the customer at the price prevailing originally. This practice is outlawed.

### Bulk Identification/Segregation

A system for segregating customer securities in accordance with SEC Rule 15c3-3 in which all certificates and/or depository positions of an issue are identified as belonging to all customers. For example, a broker has ten customers each owning 100 shares, and the broker segregates one certificate for 1,000 shares.

### Bullet Loan

Short-term financing in which the entire principal is repaid in one amount, or "bullet."

### Bullish

Describing an opinion or outlook that a rise in price is expected either in the general market or in an individual security.

*See* Bearish.

### Bull Market

A securities market characterized by rising prices.

*See* Bear Market.

### Bull Spread

An option spread so designed that a profit will result if the underlying security increases in market value. The trader buys (long) the lower strike price and sells (writes) the higher strike price.

*See* Bear Spread.

### Bunching Odd-Lot Orders

The combination of several odd-lot orders into round lots so they can be handled by a commission house broker, specialist, or two-dollar broker, thereby eliminating the odd-lot differential.

### Business Day

Defined by the Federal Reserve as any day the New York Stock Exchange is open for business.

Defined by the New York Stock Exchange as any day the New York banks are open for business.

### Butterfly Spread

An option strategy combining both limited risk and limited profit potential. It is a combination of a bull spread and a bear spread where striking prices are involved. The lower two prices are utilized in the bull spread and the higher two in the bear spread. Puts or calls can form this strategy with four different ways of combining options to construct the same basic position.

### Buy Down

A mortgage loan in which a seller or homebuilder pays an "up-front" amount to a lender, who then gives buyers below-market-rate loans, either for a period or for the life of the loan.

### Buy-In

On any day on or after a prescribed settlement date, the purchasing firm that has failed to receive the certificates can give written notice to the selling firm that the contract is in default, and (1) after giving notice, purchase the security in the marketplace, and (2) hold the seller responsible for any money loss that may be incurred.

*See* Sell-out.

### Buy Minus

A market or limit order to purchase a security at a price lower than the previous differently priced transaction for that security.

### Buyout

Purchasing a controlling percentage (if not all) of a company's stock, through either negotiation or tender offer, in order to take over its assets and operations.

### Buy Stop Order

Instructions on a buy order for a broker/specialist on the exchange floor to execute the order at the best available price when the market price touches the customer's price or when a transaction takes place above the price. Upon execution, the transaction activates (elects or triggers) the order, making it a market order to buy.

### Buy the Book

An instruction to buy, at the current offer price, all available shares from the specialist in a security and/or from other broker/dealers. This instruction usually comes from traders or institutions.

### Buyer's Option

*See* Call.

### Buyer's Option Contract

A securities contract in which the seller's delivery of the certificates is due at the purchaser's office on the date specified at the time of the transaction. For example, "Buyer's 10" means delivery is due ten calendar days after the transaction date.

*See* Cash Contract; Regular Way Contract; Seller's Option Contract; When Issued/When Distributed Contract.

### Buying Power

The dollar amount of equity securities a customer could purchase without additional funds and continue to meet the initial margin requirements of Regulation T of the Federal Reserve. Computed as Reg T excess divided by Reg T initial margin requirements.

For example: $10,000 divided by 50% = $20,000.

### BW

An abbreviation for "Bid Wanted," indicating that the broker/dealer is soliciting buyers of the stock or bond.

### Bylaws

Rules of operation for members of the association in the over-the-counter market, established and maintained by the Board of Governors of the NASD.

*See* Schedule C.

The internal rules governing the operations of a corporation.

### Cabinet Crowd

*See* Inactive Bonds.

### Cage (The)

A slang expression used to describe a location where a brokerage firm's cashier department responsibilities are satisfied.

### Calamity Call

*See* Catastrophe (Calamity) Call.

### Calendar Spread

An option strategy using the sale of a short-term option and the purchase of a longer-term option, both having the same striking price. Either puts or calls may be used.

A *calendar combination* is a strategy combining a call calendar spread and a put calendar spread, with the striking price of the calls being higher than the striking price of the puts.

A *calendar straddle* combines the selling of a near-term straddle and the purchase of a longer-term straddle, both with the same striking price.

### Calendar Straddle or Combination

*See* Calendar Spread.

### Call

An option giving its holder (buyer) the right to demand the purchase of 100 shares of stock at a fixed price any time within a specified period (the lifetime of the option). Also sometimes referred to as a buyer's option.

*See* Put.

### Call Feature

A feature of preferred stock through which it may be retired at the corporation's option by paying a price equal to or slightly higher than either the par or market value.

A bond feature by which all or part of an issue may be redeemed by the corporation before maturity and under certain specified conditions.

### Call Loan

*See* Broker's Collateral (Call) Loan.

### Call Money

*See* Broker's Collateral Loan.

### Call Money Rate

The percentage of interest a broker/dealer pays on a broker's collateral loan.

### Call Protection

A term used to describe a bond or preferred stock without a call feature or with a call feature that cannot be activated for a period of time.

### Call Provision

The right of the lender of funds to ask for prompt repayment.

### Callable

*See* Call Feature.

### Callable Preferred

Any security that may be redeemed prior to maturity at the option of the issuer for the purpose of repurchasing preferred stock.

### Called Away

A term used to describe (1) a security called by the issuer from a client's account or (2) a security that must be delivered because a short call is exercised against the client's account.

### Can Crowd

*See* Inactive Bonds.

### Cancellation

Revocation of a buy or sell order, an action that is permissible at any time prior to execution. After execution, it is allowed only with the consent of the other party to the trade and with the approval of an NYSE floor official.

### Cap (Interest Rate)

An arbitrary ceiling placed on interest rates by negotiation. Also known as "ceiling."

*See* Floor.

### Capital Gain (Loss)

Profit (or loss) from the sale of a capital asset. Capital gains may be short-term (6 months or less) or long-term (more than 6 months). Capital losses are used to offset capital gains to establish a net position for tax purposes.

### Capital Markets

The markets in which corporate securities (equity and debt) are traded, as opposed to money markets in which short-term debt instruments are traded.

### Capitalization

*See* Total Capitalization.

### Capital Stock

A corporation's total equity capital. This is a synonym for the more popular term, "common stock."

### Capital Surplus

*See* Paid-In Capital.

### Carrying Cost

Expense of the interest paid on a debit balance when a position is established.

### Cash Account

An account in a brokerage firm in which all transactions are settled on a cash basis.

### Cash Contract

A securities contract by which delivery of the certificates is due at the purchaser's office the same day as the date of the trade.

*See* Buyer's Option Contract; Regular Way Contract; Seller's Option Contract; When Issued/When Distributed Contract.

### Cash Cow

A colloquial term for any business that generates an ongoing cash flow. These businesses have well-known products and pay dividends reliably.

### Cash Dividend

Any payment made to a corporation's shareholders in cash from current earnings or accumulated profits. Cash dividends are taxable as income.

### Cash Flow

Reported net income of a corporation plus amounts charged off for depreciation, depletion, amortization, and other noncash expenses.

### Cash Flow Bond

*See* Pay-Through Bond.

### Cash Flow Yield

A monthly internal rate of return of an investment in a projected stream of monthly principal and interest payments. The yield varies with the prepayment assumption that determines the cash flow pattern.

### Cash-on-Cash

A measurement of return on investment in which the net cash earnings from a project are related to the actual cash invested.

### Cash on Delivery (COD)

*See* Delivery Versus Payment.

### Cash Trade

A transaction involving specific securities, in which the settlement date is the same as the trade date.

### Cashier Department

A department of a broker/dealer organization responsible for the physical handling of securities and money, delivery and receipt, collateral loans, borrowing, lending, and transfer of securities, and other financial transactions.

### Catastrophe (Calamity) Call

An issuer's call for redemption of a bond issue when certain events occur, such as an accident at a construction site that severely affects the completion of the project.

### CATS (Certificates of Accrual on Treasury Securities)

Issues from the U.S. Treasury sold at a deep discount from their face value. They are called *zero-coupon* securities because they require no interest payments during their lifetime, but they return the full face value at maturity. They cannot be called away.

*See* Zero-Coupon Discount Security.

### CBOE

*See* Chicago Board Options Exchange, Inc.

### CCS

*See* Central Certificate Service.

### CD

*See* Certificate of Deposit (CD).

### Cedel S.A.

With Euroclear Clearance System Ltd., one of the two main clearance organizations for international security trades (mostly Eurobonds, but some equities too).

### Central Bank

A Federal Reserve Bank situated in one of twelve banking districts in the United States.

The Federal Reserve System.

The main bank of any country.

### Central Certificate Service (CCS)

Former name of the Depository Trust Company.

### Certificate

The actual piece of paper that is evidence of ownership or creditorship in a corporation. Water-marked certificates are finely engraved with delicate etchings to discourage forgery.

### Certificates of Accrual on Treasury Securities.

*See* CATs.

### Certificate of Deposit (CD)

A negotiable money market instrument issued by commercial banks against money deposited with them for a specified period of time. CDs vary in size according to the amount of the deposit and the maturity period, and they may be redeemed before maturity only by sale in a secondary market.

### Certificate of Incorporation

A state-validated certificate recognizing a business organization as a legal corporate entity.

*See* Charter.

### Certificate of Indebtedness (CI)

A federal bearer debt instrument in denominations of $1,000 to $500 million at a fixed interest rate, with maturities up to one year; they are fully marketable at a price reflecting their average rate of return.

### Certificated Security

A security whose ownership may be represented by a physical document. Also known as being available in "definitive form."

### Chapter 7

Part of the bankruptcy law of the 1978 Act dealing with liquidation, providing for a court-appointed interim trustee with the power to change management, get financing, and run the debtor business so that no more losses occur. The debtor can regain possession from the trustee by filing an appropriate bond.

### Chapter 11

Part of the bankruptcy law of the 1978 Act dealing with reorganization. Unless the court rules differently, the debtor still owns and runs the business. In this way, the debtor and creditor can work together. The 1978 law, by relaxing the old *absolute priority rule*, enables the debtor to negotiate new payment schedules, restructure debt, and even take out new loans.

### Charter

A document written by the founders of a corporation and filed with a state. The state approves the articles and then issues a certificate of incorporation. Together, the two documents become the charter and the corporation is recognized as a legal entity. The charter includes such information as the corporation's name, purpose, amount of shares, and the identity of the directors. Internal management rules are written by the founders in the *bylaws*.

*See* Certificate of Incorporation.

### Check Kiting

The illegal practice of drawing a check upon a demand deposit account that contains no money or has insufficient funds. It is so called even if the person deposits someone else's check into his account prior to clearance of the check previously drawn and presented as payment for an obligation.

### Chicago Board Options Exchange, Inc. (CBOE)

The first national exchange to trade listed stock options.

### Chief Examiner's Department

The department of the New York Stock Exchange responsible for the auditing of member firms.

### Chinese Wall

Colloquial name given to a brokerage firm's security measures aimed at preventing the communication of sensitive information among departments.

### Churning

A registered representative's improper handling of a customer's account: He or she buys and sells securities for a customer while intent only on the amount of commissions generated, ignoring the customer's interests and objectives.

### Circle

*See* Indication of Interest.

### CL

*See* Construction Loan.

### Class

All put and call contracts on the same underlying security.

### Clean

When block positioners can match customers buy-and-sell orders for a security, they don't have to take the security into inventory. This kind of trade is said to be "clean." If the transaction appears on the exchange tape, the term "clean on the tape" is often used. Also sometimes referred to as "natural."

### Clean Opinion

*See* Qualified Legal Opinion.

### Clearance/Clear/Clearing

The delivery of securities and monies in completion of a trade.

The comparison and/or netting of trades prior to settlement.

### Clearing Bank

A bank that provides services for their custodial accounts such as, holding inventory positions, receiving and delivering securities and disbursing funds.

### Clearing House Funds

Money represented by a person's demand deposit account at a commercial bank Withdrawals are accomplished by means of a check, which notifies the bank to transfer a sum to someone else's account, or to another bank.

Funds used in settlement of equity, corporate bond, and municipal bond settlement transactions.

A term used to mean "next-day availability" of funds.

*See* Federal Funds.

### Clearing Member of the NYSE

A member organization of the NYSE whose clearance operations are handled through the Stock Clearing Corporation.

### Climax (Buying/Selling)

A large increase or decrease in the price of a security accompanied by large volume. The price change should gap, indicating a completion of a price increase or decrease cycle.

*See* Gap.

### Close

The final transaction price for an issue on the stock exchange at the end of a trading day.

### Close-Out Procedure

The procedure taken by either party to a transaction when the contrabroker defaults; the disappointed purchaser may "buy in;" and the rejected seller may "sell out" or liquidate.

*See* Reclamation; Rejection.

### Closed-End Investment Company

A management company whose equity capitalization remains constant unless special action is taken by the directors to alter it (by the issuance of new shares).

### Closed-End Provision

A mortgage bond provision in the indenture that, in the event of default or liquidation, entitles first bondholders to a claim upon assets senior to second and subsequent bondholders, whenever the same real assets are used as collateral for more than one issue of debt.

### Closing

A meeting of all concerned parties on the date of delivery of a new issue of municipal securities, usually including the representatives of the issuer, bond counsel, and the purchasers or underwriters. The issuer makes physical delivery of the signed securities, and the required legal documents are exchanged.

### Closing Quotation

A market maker's final bid and asked prices for an issue as he or she ceases trading activities at the end of the business day.

### Closing Transaction

Any trade that reduces an investor's current position.

Purchase: The purchase of a listed option so as to close or eliminate an existing short/written position.

Sale: The sale of a listed option so as to close or eliminate an existing long position.

*See* Opening Transaction.

### Closing the Underwriting Contract

The finalizing of contractual terms between an issuing corporation and the underwriters. Usually one week after the effective date, the certificates are given over to the underwriters and payment in full is made to the corporation.

### Closure, Indefinite, of Transfer Books

Under NYSE Rule 213, the exchange may direct the assignments and powers of substitution on certificates of a company whose books are closed indefinitely to be properly acknowledged.

### CMO

*See* Collateralized Mortgage Obligation.

### CNS

*See* Continuous Net Settlement.

### Code of Arbitration

Rules established and maintained by the NASD Board of Governors to regulate arbitration of intra-member and customer/member disputes involving securities transactions.

*See* Board of Arbitration.

### COD Trade

Cash on delivery. A general term to describe a transaction in which a seller is obliged to deliver securities to the purchaser or the purchaser's agent to collect payment.

### COD Transaction

A purchase of securities in behalf of a customer promising full payment immediately upon delivery of the certificates to an agent bank or broker/dealer.

### Collateral

Securities and other property pledged by a borrower to secure repayment of a loan.

### Collateralized Mortgage Obligation (CMO)

A pooled mortgage loan that is identified by issuer. CMOs are assigned not pool numbers, but rather a series designator, which differentiates each issue and the individual classes within the series. Each class (tranch) has a different coupon, maturity, and price. Each class can also have a different underlying collateral (GNMA I or II, GPM, FNMA, FHLMC or conventional). Principal and interest payments are allocated to investors semiannually. While interest is paid seminannually to each class, principal payments are paid to one class at a time in maturity order.

A mortgage-backed corporate bond (also known as fast-pay/slow-pay bonds and serialized mortgage-backed securities), characterized by multiple prioritized classes or tranches. Classes of these issues are ranked by which bonds are redeemed. A given class is not redeemed until all bonds of an earlier priority have been redeemed, thus creating a series of bonds with distinct expected maturities.

### Collateral Trust Bond

A bond issue that is protected by a portfolio of securities held in trust by a commercial bank. The bond usually requires immediate redemption if the market value of the securities drops below or close to the value of the issue.

### Collection Ratio

An analysis of the average number of days it takes a corporation to receive payment for merchandise it has sold.

### Combination

Any position, other than a straddle, involving both put and call options.

*See* Straddle.

### Commercial Paper

Unsecured, short-term (usually a maximum of nine months) bearer obligations in denominations from $100,000 to $1 million, issued principally by industrial corporations, finance companies, and commercial factors at a discount from face value.

### Commingling

The act of using various customer securities in the same loan arrangement with the firm's securities. This practice is prohibited.

### Commission

A broker's fee for handling transactions for a client in an agency capacity.

### Commission House Broker

A member of the NYSE executing orders in behalf of his or her own organization and its customers.

### Committee of Corporate Financing

A standing national committee of the NASD that examines all appropriate documents regarding the issuance of new securities, reviewing and approving their terms and conditions.

### Committee on Uniform Security Identification Procedures (CUSIP)

An agency of the NASD responsible for issuing identification numbers for virtually all publicly owned stock and bond certificates.

### Commodities Futures Trading Commission (CFTC)

Formed in 1976 by Congress, the CFTC oversees all matters of disclosure and information, registration of firms and individuals, fair trading procedures, and the maintenance of an options and futures market.

### Commodity

A bulk good that is grown or mined, such as grains or precious metals.

*See* Futures.

### Common Stock

A unit of equity ownership in a corporation. Owners of this kind of stock exercise control over corporate affairs and enjoy any capital appreciation. They are paid dividends only after preferred stock. Their interest in the assets, in the event of liquidation, is junior to all others.

### Common Stock Equivalents

Debt and/or equity securities capable of subscription, exchange, or conversion into common stock of the company.

Convertible bonds and convertible preferred stock may be so classified at the time of issuance, based on many factors. Once so classified, they must be considered as common stock when computing primary earnings per share.

### Common Stock Ratio

The relationship of common stock outstanding to the total capitalization of a corporation.

### Comparison

A confirmation of a contractual agreement citing terms and conditions of a transaction between broker/dealers. This document must be exchanged by the contra firms shortly after trade date.

*See* Confirmation.

### Competitive Bidding

A sealed envelope bidding process employed by various underwriter groups interested in handling the distribution of a securities issue. The contract is awarded to one group by the issuer on the basis of the highest price paid, interest rate expense, and tax considerations.

### Competitive Trader

A member of an organized exchange who may, subject to certain rules and restrictions, trade for his or her own account and risk while on the trading floor.

### Compliance Department

A department of a stock exchange whose function is to oversee market activity and to ensure that all trading complies with SEC regulations. Any company that does not comply may be delisted, and a trader/brokerage house in violation may be barred from the exchange.

### Concession

In a municipal bond offering, the underwriters may offer a dollar discount from the offering price to MSRB members who are not taking part in the underwriting but who buy for their own or customers' accounts.

In a corporate underwriting, the underwriters may extend a dollar remuneration for each share or bond to selling group members who market the securities successfully.

### Conditional Prepayment Rate (CPR)

In mortgage-backed trading, prepayment rate that assumes that each month a constant proportion of outstanding mortgages will prepay.

### Conduit

Under NASD interpretations regarding hot issues, "conduit" refers to undisclosed affiliations with a bank, trust, or a similar organization.

### Conduit Financing

Securities issued by a governmental unit to help finance a project. The monies are used primarily by a third party, usually a corporation engaged in private enterprise. (Industrial development bonds are a common type of conduit financing.) The security for this issue is usually the credit of the private user rather than the governmental issuer, and the corporate obligar is usually liable for generating the pledged revenues.

### Conduit Theory

*See* Pipeline (Conduit) Theory.

### Confidence Theory

A market theory stating that stock price movements are affected by increases or decreases in investor confidence in economic trends in the country.

*See* Barron's Confidence Index.

### Confirmation

An announcement of transaction terms and conditions and other pertinent information that is prepared for customer trade activities. It serves as a bill for customer purchases and as an advisory notice for sales.

### Conflict of Interest

A legal term used to describe the situation in which a person or group of people is placed in position of authority so that they may personally profit from a disservice to those to whom they are responsible.

### Congestion Area

In technical analysis, a period of trading during which the market reacts in alternating directions with great frequency. This area is characterized by small peaks and dips without any clear trend in either direction.

### Consolidated Tape

A system of reporting all trades in New York Stock Exchange listed securities on one tape, called Tape A, and all other exchange-listed securities on another tape, called Tape B, regardless of where the trade takes place.

### Constant Dollar Plan

Similar to a constant ratio plan, this is an investment plan by which an investor keeps a constant dollar value of different securities in his or her portfolio—either through purchases and sales or by depositing additional funds as necessary.

*See* Constant Ratio Plan.

### Constant Dollars (C$)

Dollars used as a benchmark value when comparing the value of money from year to year. The "constant dollars" are usually the dollars, and associated value, of an arbitrarily selected year.

### Constant Ratio Plan

A formula investment plan requiring a fixed percentage balance between stocks and bonds in a portfolio. The ratio is determined by the owner's investment objectives, and purchases and sales are effected to maintain the predetermined percentages.

*See* Constant Dollar Plan.

### Construction and Development REIT

An REIT primarily engaged in providing to builders short-term financing during the construction period of a project.

### Construction Loan (CL)

Short-term construction financing covering the period from the start of a project to its completion, but prior to opening. Funds are advanced as needed to pay contractors, and interest is paid only on the funds used. Upon completion, it usually is replaced by a long-term loan.

*See* Take-Out Loan.

A loan made to a project developer that eventually becomes a project loan. CLs are backed by GNMAs.

### Consumer Credit

Credit extended to the ultimate users of goods and services.

### Contingent Order

One order given to the trading desk of a brokerage firm to buy stock and then sell a covered call option. Also called a "net order" and a "not held" order.

*See* Market Not Held Order, Switch (Contingent or Swap) Order.

### Contingent Rate

A rate of interest subject to change upon the occurrence of an event that is foreseeable but that is not certain to occur.

### Continuing Commissions

The practice of paying commissions to registered representatives after they have left the employment of the broker/dealer or to their heirs after a registered representative has died.

### Continuous Net Settlement (CNS)

A procedure used by all clearing corporations to simplify processing daily transactions and correspondingly to reduce the number of certificate deliveries required. The clearing corporation interposes itself on each transaction, crediting or debiting each member's total holding in each issue. The net balance is carried forward from day to day.

### Contrabroker (Contra Side)

A term used to describe the broker with whom a trade was made.

### Contract Grade

A commodity grade that an exchange officially designates as acceptable for delivery in a futures contract settlement.

### Contract Market

A board of trade that the Commodity Futures Trading Commission specifies as the market for a given commodity.

### Contract Sheet

A complete list of each member's daily transactions arranged by issue and prepared by the clearing house for members to check for accuracy of detail and approval of settlement terms.

### Contractual (Periodic Payment) Plan

An investment plan for a mutual fund by which an investor agrees to invest a fixed sum of money at specified intervals over a 10- or 15-year period.

*See* Front-End (Prepaid Charge) Plan.

### Controller's Department

The department of any business responsible for keeping the accounting records, preparing and filing reports with various government and regulatory bodies, and preparing financial reports for management.

### Control Person

A person subject to special rules of the SEC when acquiring or selling control stock. A control person is one who: (1) owns or controls 10% or more of the voting stock of a corporation; (2) holds a position as an officer or director of a corporation; or (3) is in a position to influence the decision-making process of a corporation.

### Control Stock

Stock owned by a control person in the corporation over which he or she has control.

### Conventional Mortgage

A mortgage, other than one insured by the Federal Housing Administration (FHA) or guaranteed by the Veterans Administration (VA).

### Conventional Option

An option contract entered into by two parties that is not standardized as to striking price and/or expiration date and is not cleared through the Options Clearing Corporation.

An over-the-counter or unlisted option.

### Conversion

A bond feature by which the owner may exchange his or her bonds for a specified number of shares of stock. Interest paid on such bonds is lower than the usual interest rate for straight debt issues.

*See* Conversion Parity; Conversion Price; Conversion Ratio.

A feature of some preferred stock by which the owner is entitled to exchange preferred for common stock, usually of the same company, in accordance with the terms of the issue.

A feature of some mutual fund offerings allowing an investor to exchange shares for comparable value in another fund with different objectives handled by the same management group.

A term used to describe the creation of a call option from a put option by means of taking a long position in the underlying equity.

### Conversion Arbitrage

A transaction where the arbitrageur buys the underlying security, but then buys a put and sells a call, both of which options have the same terms.

*See* Reversal Arbitrage.

### Conversion Parity

The equal dollar relationship between a convertible security and the underlying stock trading at or above the conversion price.

### Conversion Price (Value)

In the case of convertible bonds, the price of the underlying common stock at which conversion can be made. The price is set by the issuing corporation and is printed in the indenture.

The value created by changing from one form to another. An example would be the added property value when an investor changes rental properties to condominiums.

### Conversion Ratio

The ratio indicating how many underlying shares may be obtained upon exchange of each convertible security.

*See* Convertible Security.

### Converted Put

*See* Synthetic Put.

### Convertible Bond

Bond that can be exchanged for a specified number of another security, usually shares, at a prestated price. Convertibility typically enhances the bond's marketability.

### Convertible Funds

A type of mutual fund in which the investor purchases bonds or preferred stocks containing an option allowing the owner to convert at any time to a specified number of common shares of the insurer. This type of mutual fund can offer current income as well as capital gain potential.

### Convertible Preferred Stock

*See* Conversion.

### Convertible (Security)

Any security that can be converted into another security. For example, a convertible bond or convertible preferred stock may be converted into the underlying stock of the same corporation at a fixed rate. The rate at which the shares of the bond or preferred stock are converted into the common is called the conversion ratio.

### Cooling-Off Period

*See* Twenty-Day (Cooling-Off) Period.

### Co-Op

*See* Banks for Cooperatives.

### Cornering the Market

A situation in which a party or group has acquired a substantial quantity of the available shares and, as a result, exerts considerable influence on the shares' market price.

### Corporate Bond Equivalent Yield

In mortgage-backed trading, an upward adjustment to reflect the monthly payment of interest rather than the semiannual payment of interest, which is the convention in the corporate and government bond markets.

For whole loans, an adjustment to mortgage yield calculations necessary to compare mortgage assets to alternative investments such as Treasury Notes, corporate bonds, CMOs and other semiannual paying bonds. This adjustment compensates for monthly compounding.

### Corporation

A business organization chartered by a state secretary as a recognized legal institution of and by itself and operated by an association of individuals, with the purpose of ensuring perpetuity and limited financial liability.

*See* Certificate of Incorporation; Charter.

### Correspondent

A bank or other financial institution that performs services for another in a market or in an area that the other does not have access to.

### Cost of Goods Sold

The expense of inventory marketed in a particular accounting period.

### Counter

A response to a bid, offer, market or order, giving an alternative price at which the responder is willing to do business. A counter ordinarily turns a firm bid, offer, or market into a subject one.

### Counterfeit Securities

SEC Rule 17f-1 states that any reporting institution is obliged to report the discovery of any counterfeit security to the appropriate instrumentality and the appropriate law enforcement agency within one business day of such a discovery.

### Coupon Bond

A bond with interest coupons attached. The coupons are clipped as they come due and are presented by the holders to their banks for payment.

*See* Bearer Bond; Registered Bond.

### Coupon Yield

*See* Nominal Yield.

### Cover (Covering)

To buy back an initially written option as a closing transaction.

To buy a security previously sold short to eliminate that open position.

### Covered Straddle Write

The strategy in which an investor owns the underlying security but also writes a straddle on that security.

### Covered Write

The writing or selling of a call option or put against a position in the underlying stock or its equivalent. A short call is covered if the underlying stock is owned. A short put is covered if the underlying stock is also short in the account.

### CPR

*See* Conditional Prepayment Rate.

### Credit

Time allowed for the payment of goods and services.

Power to buy or borrow on trust.

In bookkeeping the right-hand side of an account, as opposed to a debit. It is all monies received in an account. A credit transaction is made when the net sale proceeds are larger than the net buy proceeds (cost), thereby bringing money into the account.

*See* Debit.

A deposit against which one may draw.

### Credit Agreement

A document containing the complete terms and arrangements by which financing will be conducted in a customer's account. It emphasizes when and how interest is charged for the lending service provided.

### Credit Balance

In a customer's account of a broker/dealer, the credit balance indicates that the broker/dealer owes money to the customer either conditionally or unconditionally.

The opposite of debit balance.

### Credit Department

*See* Margin (Credit) Department.

### Cross (Crossing Stock)

A broker/dealer's pairing off of a purchase order with a sell order in the same security at the same time and price for different customers.

### Crossed Market

Situation in which a broker's bid is higher than the lowest offer of another broker or vice versa. NASD rules for NASD Automated Quotations forbid dealers to intentionally cross the market.

### Cross-Over Price

The price at which outstanding securities are refinanced.

*See* Cross-Over Refunding.

### Cross-Over Refunding

A procedure by which outstanding securities are refinanced through the proceeds of a new issue of securities prior to the date when the outstanding securities become due or are callable.

### Cross-Over Yield

The yield created by cross-over refunding.

### Cross Rate

The exchange rate between two foreign currencies. Usually the U.S. dollar is not one of the two currencies, but it is used in determining the cross rate. For example, to exchange yen for francs, you would sell yen against the dollar and buy francs with those dollars.

### Crowd

*See* Trading Crowd.

### Crummey Trust

A trust set up so that a minor has the right to withdraw money.

### Cum Dividend

A term applied to stock at a time when the purchaser will be entitled to a forthcoming dividend.

### Cum Rights

A term applied to a stock trading in the marketplace "with subscription rights attached," which are reflected in the price of that security.

### Cumulative Preferred Stock

A preferred stock that accrues any omitted dividends as a claim against the company. This claim must be paid in full before any dividends may be paid on the company's common stock.

### Cumulative Voting

A voting privilege that allows a stockholder to multiply the shares she or he owns by the number of vacancies to be filed on the board (or proposals to be resolved). The stockholder can then apportion his or her total votes accordingly in the manner he or she prefers. This procedure is particularly advantageous for minority stockholders.

### Curbstone Broker

A trader for the American Stock Exchange.

### Currency Futures

Futures contracts on foreign currencies, such as U.S. dollars, British pounds, French francs, Deutsche marks, Swiss francs, or Japanese yen. They provide hedging capability to corporations who sell their products internationally.

### Currency in Circulation

Paper bills and coins used by the general public to pay for goods and services.

### Current Asset

Cash or an item of value expected to be converted into cash within one year or one operating cycle, whichever is longer.

### Current Liability

An obligation of a corporation payable within one year or one operating cycle, whichever is longer.

### Current Market Value

According to Regulation T of the Federal Reserve Board, the latest closing price (or quotation, if no sale occurred).

According to NYSE rules, the up-to-the-minute last sale price of a security.

### Current Ratio

Current assets divided by current liabilities. Also known as working capital ratio.

### Current Yield

The annual dollar interest paid by a bond divided by its market price. It is the actual return rate, not the coupon rate. Example: Any bond carrying a 6% coupon and trading at 95 is said to offer a current yield of 6.3% ($60 coupon ÷ $950 market price = 6.3%). Also sometimes referred to as current yield to maturity.

*See* Nominal Yield.

### Cushion Bond

A higher-than-current coupon debt instrument with a deferred call provision in its indenture offering a better current return and minimal price volatility (as compared with a bond without call protection). It normally trades with large premiums.

### Cushion Theory of Investment

A theory of investment that views the short seller as a stabilizing influence on either a bull or bear market.

### CUSIP

*See* Committee on Uniform Security Identification Procedure.

### CUSIP Number

A unique identifying number appearing on the face of publicly traded securities.

### Custodian

A person or institution legally charged with the responsibility of safeguarding the property of another.

### Custodial Agreement

The agreement for the retention of each Mortgage Note, Mortgage & Assignment of Mortgage annexed hereto as Exhibit D.

### Customer

For purposes of disclosure of financial condition under SEC Rule 17a-5, a customer is any person for whom, or with whom, the broker/dealer firm (1) has executed a transaction, or (2) holds or owes monies or securities for that month or the month following for which the firm's financial report is to be prepared.

### Customer's Agreement

A document that explains the terms and conditions under which a brokerage firm consents to finance a customer's credit transaction. No margin account should be opened or maintained unless the customer signs such an agreement. Also known as margin agreement or hypothecation agreement.

### CV

Abbreviation for "convertible."

### Cycle

The cyclical four-month expiration dates applied to various classes of options, such as January/April/July/October (JAJO).

### Cyclical Stock

Any stock, such as housing industry-related stock, that tends to rise in price quickly when the economy turns up and fall quickly when the economy turns down.

### DAC

*See* Deliver Versus Payment.

### Daily Trading Limit

A maximum that many options or commodities are permitted to fall or rise in one trading day. Most exchanges impose a daily trading limit on each contract.

### Daisy Chain

A series of purchases and sales of the same issue at successively higher (or lower) prices, by the same group of people. Its purpose is to manipulate prices and draw unsuspecting investors into the market, leaving them defrauded of their money or securities.

### Dated Date

With regard to bonds and other debt instruments, the date from which interest is determined to accrue, upon the sale of the security. The buyer pays the amount equal to the interest accrued from the dated date to the settlement date and is reimbursed with the first interest payment on the security.

### Date of Record

The date set by the corporate board of directors for the transfer agent to close the agency's books to further changes in registration of stock and to identify the recipients of a forthcoming distribution. Also known as record date.

*See* Ex-Dividend Date.

The date on which you must be registered as a holder of a debt security to be entitled to payment of principal and interest. The record date falls on the last business day of the month.

In mortgage-backed securities, the close of business on the last day of the month preceding the month of the related remittance date. (If the last day is not a business day, the business day immediately preceding such last day.)

### Day Order

A transaction order that remains valid only for the remainder of the trading day on which it is entered.

### Day Trading

The act of buying and selling a position during the same day.

### Dealer

An individual or firm in the securities business acting as a principal rather than as an agent.

*See* As Agent; As Principal.

### Dealer Bank

A commercial bank's offering of a market in government or agency securities.

A bank department registered as a municipal securities dealer with the MSRB.

### Dealer Book

A publication by *The Bond Buyer* issued semiannually listing municipal bond dealers, municipal finance consultants, and bond attorneys within the United States. The book is colloquially referred to as the "red book" (the color of its cover), but it is really entitled *Directory of Municipal Bond Dealers of the United States*. Standard & Poor's Corporation prints a similar book entitled *Securities Dealers of North America*, which includes Canadian dealers.

### Debenture

An unsecured debt offering by a corporation, promising only the general assets as protection for creditors. Sometimes the so-called "general assets" are only goodwill and reputation.

### Debit

Money paid out of an account. In a debit transaction, the net cost is greater than the net sale proceeds.

*See* Credit.

### Debit Balance

The balance owed by a customer in his or her account as reflected on the brokerage firm's ledger statement of settled transactions.

### Debt/Equity Ratio

The ratio of long-term debt to shareholders' equity.

### Debt Instrument

The document specifying the terms and conditions of a loan between a lender and a borrower.

### Debt Security

Any security reflecting the loan of money that must be paid back to the lender in the future, such as a bill, note, or bond.

### Deep Discount Bond

A bond, although issued at par, that is currently selling below 80 percent of its par value. *Not* a bond sold at an original issue discount.

*See* Discount Bond.

### Deep in the Money

A term used to describe a securities option with a strike price that is already profitable and relatively far from the market price of the underlying security. The option has intrinsic value.

In certain regulatory contexts, more than 5 points in the money.

### Deep Out of the Money

A term used to describe a securities option with a strike price that is unprofitable and relatively far from the market price of the underlying security.

In certain regulatory contexts, more than 5 points out of the money.

### Deep Pocket

The financial condition of partners in a venture with all but inexhaustible funds.

### Default

The failure of a corporation to pay principal and/or interest on outstanding bonds or dividends on its preferred stock.

### Defeasance

The substitution of a new debt for old debt. Specifically, a corporation replaces old, low-rate debt with securities having less face value but paying a higher interest.

A company could also have a broker/dealer buy up its bonds and convert them to a new issue of the company's stock, which is of equal value to the bonds. The broker can later sell the stock for a profit.

### Deferred Charge

Expenses incurred by a corporation to improve or promote the long-term prospects of business. They may be apportioned and charged off against earnings over a period of years.

### Deficiency Letter

A letter from the SEC to an issuer stating the nature of material omissions or misrepresentations in the corporation's registration statement. The effective date is postponed until such deficiencies are corrected.

### Definitive Form

*See* Certified Security.

### Delay

In mortgage-backed trading, the "stated" time elapsed to the *first* payment of principal and interest (GNMAs—45 days, FHLM CPCs—75 days, FNMA MBSs—54 days, conventional pass-throughs—54 days). The "actual" delay, or penalty, is 30 days less than the "stated" delay.

### Delay Days

In whole loans, a period created by the mortgage-servicing process, whereby the servicer has the use of mortgage cash flows and the investor is not paid accrued interest. To compensate them for the lost float, investors get a reduced purchase price that represents the present value of the opportunity cost for the lost float.

### Delayed Delivery

The settlement of a securities contract, by mutual agreement, at some date later than that for regular way delivery, which is usually the next business day, whereas a delayed delivery could be held off for one more business day.

### Delayed Opening

The delay of the opening of trading in a security when buy and sell orders are grossly out of balance with each other.

### Deliver

In options trading, transferring securities from one individual's or firm's account to another individual's or firm's account. The assigned call writer must deliver the stock to the exercised call holder. An exercised put holder must deliver the stock to the assigned put writer.

### Delivery Date

The day delivery of securities is made, which may be on or subsequent to settlement date.

### Delivery Instructions

Delivery information for a trade, used in settlement, that indicate where securities should be delivered or received.

### Delivery (Deliverable) Grade

*See* Contract Grade.

### Delivery Notice

The date on a futures contract when the actual commodity is to be delivered to the buyer.

A formal notice documenting when the goods will be delivered.

### Delivery Versus Payment

The purchase of securities in a cash account with instructions that payment will be made immediately upon the delivery of the securities, sometimes to the contra broker but usually to an agent bank. Also known as "deliver against cash" (DAC).

*See* COD Trade.

### Delta

The amount that an option's price will change for a corresponding change in price of the underlying stock. Call options have positive deltas, while put options have negative deltas. The delta can be altered for even fractional changes in the underlying stock. The terms *up delta* and *down delta* describe the option's change after a full one-point change in price by the underlying security either up or down. The up delta may be larger than the down delta for a call option, while the reverse is true for put options.

*See* Hedge Ratio.

### Delta Spread

A ratio spread established as a neutral position. This neutral ratio is found by dividing the delta of the purchased option by the delta of the written option.

*See* Ratio Spread; Delta.

### Demand Deposit

A loan or checking account that gives its owner the right to withdraw funds from a commercial bank at his or her own discretion.

### Depletion Reserve

Obsolete term for allowance for depletion.

### Depository Trust Company (DTC)

An independent corporation owned by broker/dealers and banks responsible for: (1) holding deposit securities owned by broker/dealers and banking institutions; (2) arranging the receipt and delivery of securities between users by means of debiting and crediting their respective accounts; (3) arranging for payment of monies between users in the settlement of transactions. The DTC is generally used by option writers because it guarantees delivery of underlying securities if assignment is made against securities held in DTC.

### Depth

The amount of general investor interest in the market, comparing the number of issues traded with the number of issues listed: the more that are traded, the greater the "depth" of the market.

The "depth" of a security depends on how large a buy or sell order it can absorb without its price changing greatly.

### Descending Tops

In technical analysis, a chart pattern element in which each new high price for a security is lower than the preceding high—indicating a bearish trend.

### Descending Triangle

A major chart pattern in technical analysis indicating consecutive highs until a leveling-off point is reached.

### Designated Concession

An order for a number of securities given to a syndicate that designates the concessions for the nonmembers of the account. For example, nonmember A gets 1,000 out of an order for 2,000 securities; nonmember B gets 750, and nonmeber C, 250.

### Designated Order Turnaround (DOT)

A computerized system used by the New York Stock Exchange to match and automatically execute small market orders.

### Diagonal Spread

Any spread created in which (1) the purchased options have a longer maturity than do the written options and (2) both options have different striking prices. Some types of diagonal spreads are diagonal bull spreads, diagonal bear spreads, and diagonal butterfly spreads.

### Differential (Differential Return)

The dealer's compensation for handling an odd-lot transaction. The dealer adds the differential to the price of the first possible round-lot sale and fills a customer's buy order at that somewhat higher price (or at a somewhat lower price for sell order). The differential is generally one-eighth of a point and is not itemized separately on the trade confirmation.

### Digest of Earnings Reports

A section in the *Wall Street Journal* reporting in summary form the earnings of publicly held corporations soon after the information has been released.

### Digits Deleted

An announcement to signify that trade information is falling one minute behind activity on the trading floor. Only the last digit and fraction of a transaction price are then printed until the tape catches up with its timely reporting responsibilities.

### Digits Resumed

An announcement stating that the condition of digits deleted is no longer in effect.

### Dint

Also known as a "lookback" option. A lookback *put* allows its owner the right to sell the underlying commodity at the highest price achieved over a certain period. A lookback *call* allows its owner the right to purchase the underlying commodity at the lowest price achieved over a certain period.

### Dip

Any slight drop in security prices during an ongoing upward trend. It is advisable to buy on dips when the price is temporarily low.

### Direct

Any commercial paper issuer with its own marketing organization for selling paper directly to investors without the services of a commercial payer dealer. These are generally large finance companies like General Motors Acceptance Corp.

### Direct Placement

Any direct sale of securities to one or more investors, typically life insurance companies.

### Discount

Term used to describe an option trading for less than its intrinsic value.

*See* Intrinsic Value; Parity.

A term used to describe debt instruments trading at a price below their face values. For example, trading at 99 would mean that for $990 one could purchase a bond that would pay $1,000 principal at maturity.

### Discount Arbitrage

An arbitrage in which a discount option is purchased while an opposite position is taken in the underlying security.

*Basic Call Arbitrage*: The arbitrageur can buy a call at a discount and simultaneously sell the underlying stock.

*Basic Put Arbitrage:* The arbitrageur buys a put at a discount and simultaneously buys the underlying stock. Both positions are considered riskless.

*See* Discount.

### Discount Bond

A bond that sells in the marketplace at a price below its face value.

*See* Deep Discount Bond; Premium Bond.

### Discount Broker

A broker/dealer whose commission rates for buying and selling securities are markedly lower than those of a full-service broker. These brokers usually provide execution-only services.

### Discount Note

A note, originally sold at par, selling below its par value. A note is usually a government security.

## Discount Rate (The)

A rate of interest associated with borrowing reserves from a central bank by member banks in the Federal Reserve district. The rate is set by the officials of that central bank.

## Discount Security

A security sold on the basis of a bank rate discount. The investment return is realized solely from the accretion of this discounted amount to the security's maturity value. The most common type is a U.S. Treasury bill.

## Discount Window

A teller-like cage at which member banks may borrow reserves from the Federal Reserve Bank upon pledge of acceptable collateral.

## Discretion

*See* Limit Order; Market Not Held Order.

## Discretionary Account

A customer's account in which an employee of a member firm has authority to act arbitrarily. This term does not authorize the use of judgment as to time or price of execution for an order prompted by a customer.

## Discretionary Order

An order that empowers a registered representative or other brokerage firm employee to use his or her own judgment on the customer's behalf with respect to choice of security, quantity of security, and whether any such transaction should be a purchase or sale.

*See* Discretionary Account; Fractional Discretionary Order.

## Disintermediation

The effect, during periods of high interest rates, when individuals withdraw deposits from banks (which act as "intermediaries" by taking deposits and investing the funds in securities) and invest directly in securities themselves.

## Disproportionate in Quantity

Under the NASD interpretation of hot issues, certain customers may not be allocated securities disproportionately to those allocated to bona fide public customers.

## Dist

An exchange distribution as indicated on exchange ticker tapes.

*See* Exchange Distribution.

### Distributor

*See* Underwriter.

### Distribution

The sale of a large block of stock, through either an underwriting or an exchange distribution.

### Distribution Area

In technical analysis, a relatively narrow price range for a security for a long period, typically a month or more.

### Distribution Stock

Publicly sold stock offered by persons affiliated with the issuer pursuant to an effective shelf registration.

### District Bank

One of the twelve Federal Reserve Banks acting as the central bank for its district.

### District Business Conduct Committee

An NASD district subcommittee responsible for supervising and enforcing the Board of Governors' Rules of Fair Practice; it consists of the officials of the district committee itself.

### District Committee

The governing body of each of the 13 districts of the NASD.

### District Uniform Practices Committee

One of 13 district committees within the NASD whose function is the dissemination of information regarding the Uniform Practice Code.

### Diversification

Spreading investment and contingent risks among different companies in different fields of endeavor.

Investing in the securities of one company that owns or has holdings in other companies.

Investing in a fund with a portfolio containing many securities.

*See* Diversified Common Stock Company; Diversified Management Company.

### Diversified Common Stock Company

A diversified management company that invests substantially all of its assets in a portfolio of common stocks in a wide variety of industries.

### Diversified Management Company

A management company that has at least 75% of its assets represented by: (1) cash and cash items, (2) government securities, (3) securities of other investment companies, and (4) other securities, limited to securities of one issue having a value not greater than 5% of the management company's total assets and no more than 10% of the voting securities of the issuing corporation.

### Divergence

In technical analysis, when market indicators point to different trends.

### Divestiture

Disposing of assets by selling them, having employees purchase them, or otherwise liquidating them.

### Dividend Arbitrage

A riskless arbitrage in which a put is purchased along with the underlying stock. The put is purchased when it has a time value premium less than the impending dividend payment by the underlying stock and is closed after the stock goes ex-dividend.

A form of risk arbitrage in which a similar procedure is followed except that the amount of the impending dividend is unknown and therefore risk is involved in the transaction.

*See* Ex-Dividend Date; Time Value Premium.

### Dividend Payout

The percentage of dividends distributed in terms of what is available out of current net income.

### Dividends

Distributions to stockholders declared by the corporate board of directors.

### Dividends Payable

A current liability showing the amount due to stockholders for dividends declared but not yet paid.

### DK

A slang expression for "Don't Know," as applied to a securities transaction on which transactional data is missing when the brokers exchange comparison sheets. Also called a "QT" for a "questioned trade."

### Dollar Bonds

Corporate or municipal serial bonds that are denominated and that trade in currency values instead of as a percentage of face amount because of the relatively small amounts available for each maturity in the entire issue.

### Dollar Cost Averaging

A long-term investment plan based on investing fixed dollar amounts at periodic intervals, regardless of fluctuations in the prices of securities.

### DNR

*See* Do Not Reduce (DNR) Order.

### Do Not Reduce (DNR) Order

A limit order to buy, a stop order to sell, or a stop-limit order to sell that is not to be reduced by the amount of a cash dividend on the ex-dividend date because the customer specifically requested that it be entered that way.

### Dont

An option that is the same as a regular call or put except that the buyer does not pay a premium. If the option is not exercised, the buyer pays a cancellation fee. (Abbreviation taken from the French verb, *donner*, to give.)

### Don't Fight the Tape

Colloquial expression meaning, "Don't trade against the market trend."

### Don't Know

*See* DK.

### DOT

*See* Designated Order Turnaround.

### Double-Barrelled Bond

Usually municipal revenue bonds, secured by both a defined source of revenue plus the full faith and credit of an issuer with taxing powers.
*See* Overlapping Debt.

### Double Bottom

In technical analysis, a chart pattern showing that the price of a security has twice declined to its support level and risen again. It indicates that there is a demand for securities at that level and that the security shouldn't drop any farther.

### Double Declining Balance Depreciation

A highly accelerated procedure for reducing a corporation's cost basis of a qualified asset during its useful life. A significant amount is charged off against earnings during the early years of operation.

### Double Top

In technical analysis, a chart pattern showing that the price of a security has twice risen to its resistance level and fallen back. It indicates that there is a supply of securities at that level and that the security, in trying to move higher, is running into resistance at that price.

### Dow-Jones Average

A market average indicator consisting (individually) of (1) 30 industrial, (2) 20 transportation, and (3) 15 public utility common stocks; the composite average includes these 65 stocks collectively.

### Down and Out Option

A block of at least ten call options with the same striking price and expiration date that carries a provision for immediate cancellation of the exercise privilege if the underlying stock declines by a predetermined, agreed-upon amount in the marketplace.

### Down Delta

*See* Delta.

### Downgrade

Lowering a bond rating by a rating service, such as Moody's or Standard & Poor's.

### Downtick

The sale of a listed security at a lower price than that of the last regular-way transaction. For example, if a stock last sold at 27, the next regular-way transaction at 26⅞ is said to be a downtick.

### Downside Protection

In the case of a covered call, the cushion against loss if the underlying stock declines in price. Alternatively, it may be expressed in terms of the distance the stock could fall before the total position becomes a loss or an amount equal to the option premium. It can also be expressed as a percentage of the current stock price.

*See* Covered Call Write.

### Dow Theory

A theory predicated on the belief that the rise or fall of stock prices is both a mirror and a forecaster of business activities.

### Draft

A debt instrument payable on sight, or at a specific future time, upon presentation to a paying agent, usually a bank.

### Drawdown Schedule

In a construction project, the schedule showing the periodic payments or "draws" to which the contractor is entitled.

### DTC

*See* Depository Trust Company.

### Dual Purpose (Leveraged) Companies

Closed-end investment companies that initially distribute two classes of securities in equal amounts in a single offering, each class having different objectives and privileges: income shares and capital shares. Holders of either class of shares receive a benefit from at least $2 worth of portfolio for each $1 of personal investment.

### Due Bill

A document evidencing the fact that one party owes another a dividend or other distribution.

### Due Bill Check

A due bill that relates only to a cash dividend on stock or to accrued interest on registered bonds. It is a post-dated check depositable on the corporation's payment debt.

### Due Date

The day of the month on which the monthly payment is due on a mortgage loan.

### Due Diligence Meeting

A meeting between corporation officials and the underwriting group to (1) discuss the registration statement, (2) prepare a final prospectus, and (3) negotiate a formal underwriting agreement.

### Due-on-Sale Clause

In a loan agreement, a clause that calls for payment of the remaining loan balance upon a sale or other transfer of title of the underlying collateral, such as real estate.

### Dumping

In the securities market, the offering of large amounts of stock without regard for the effects on prices or the market.

In international finance, the selling of goods overseas below cost to get rid of a surplus or to gain a competitive edge on foreign firms.

### Duration

A measure of price volatility.

In mortgage-backed securities trading, a measure of an instrument's price sensitivity to changes in yields. To calculate it, take a weighted average of the periods to receipt of the cash flows (present value).

For whole loans, duration is calculated as the present value, time-weighted measure of all cash flows scheduled or expected to be received from an asset or paid on a liability.

### Duration Variability

A measure of how much the duration of a cash flow may vary from its expected value, owing to fluctuation in yields and/or prepayment rates.

### Dutch Auction

Auction in which the sellers offer down for a purchase instead of the buyers bidding up. This term is often used incorrectly to describe the weekly T-bill auction.

### DVP

*See* Delivery Versus Payment.

### Dynamic

A term used to describe option strategies analyses made during the course of changing stock prices over time, as opposed to an analysis made at expiration of the options used in the strategy. A dynamic breakeven point or a dynamic follow-up action changes as time passes.

*See* Breakeven Point; Follow-Up Action.

### Each Way

Term applied to the commission a broker makes when involved on both the purchase and sale sides of a trade.

### E & OE

Errors and omissions excepted. This legend often appears on a customer's statement. It is intended to absolve the firm of liability if it makes a mistake in preparing that statement.

### Early Exercise (Assignment)

Exercising (assigning) an option contract before the expiration date. Most options are exercised at or very close to their expiration date.

### Early Warning System

A system of financial reports made by broker/dealers under various exchange and SEC rules designed to provide information on the broker/dealer's financial condition.

### Earned Income

For federal income tax purposes, personal service income earned through salary, wages, and the like.

### Earned Surplus

*See* Retained Earnings.

### Earnest Money

Also known as "margin," the money deposited to assure a contractual commitment in futures and options trading.

### Earnings per Share

The amount of new profit attributable to each share of common stock outstanding.

### Earnings Report (Income Statement; Profit and Loss Statement)

A financial statement issued by a company showing its revenues and expenses over a given period.

### Eastern Account

*See* Severally and Jointly.

### Easy Money

A situation in which the Federal Reserve System allows banks to accumulate enough funds to lower interest rates and make borrowing easier. Easy money fosters economic growth and inflation.

*See* Tight Money.

### ECU

*See* European Currency Unit.

### Edge Act

A 1919 federal law allowing commercial banks the right to conduct international business across state lines.

### Edge Act Corporation

A federal- or state-chartered subsidiary involved with foreign lending operations.

*See* Edge Act.

### Effective Date

The date on which a security can be offered publicly if no deficiency letter is submitted to the issuer by the SEC. It is generally no earlier than the twentieth calendar day after filing the registration statement.

### Effective Lifetime

The period for which an order is valid.

### Effective Sale

A round-lot transaction consummated on the floor of the New York Stock Exchange after entry of an odd-lot order by a customer. Its price is used to determine the execution price for the odd-lot order after consideration of the dealer's fee.

*See* Differential.

### Efficient Market Hypothesis

A theory stating that market prices reflect the knowledge and expectations of all investors. Seeking undervalued stocks or forecasting any kind of market movement is futile because new developments are already reflected in the corporation's stock price, making it impossible to beat the market. Making the right investment is based purely on chance.

### Efficient Portfolio

A portfolio, arrived at mathematically, with a maximum expected return for any level of risk or a minimum level of risk for any expected return.

### Either/Or Order

*See* Alternative (Either/Or) Order.

### Electing Sale

The round-lot transaction that activates (triggers) a stop order.

### Eligible Security

A security that:

can be traded by exchange members on the OTC market even though it is listed on the exchange;

is accepted at the discount window for loans;

has a loan value under Regulation T;

can act as collateral for short option positions if deposited at the Options Clearing Corporation.

### Equalizing Sales

A minus or zero-minus short sale permitted on a national exchange by the SEC if it constitutes a plus or zero-plus tick on the principal exchange where that issue is also traded.

### Equipment Trust Bond

A serial bond collateralized by the machinery and/or equipment of the issuing corporation.

### Equity

The ownership interest in a company of holders of its common and preferred stock.

The excess of value of securities over the debit balance in a margin (general) account.

### Equity REIT

An REIT primarily engaged in taking an equity position in property.

### Equity Requirement

In options trading the minimum required amount of equity that must be present in a margin account. The normal requirement is $2,000, but some brokerage firms may impose higher equity requirements for uncovered option writing.

A prerequisite dollar amount imposed by an exchange, clearing corporation, or a brokerage firm for certain types of transactions.

### Equity Self-Funding Point

In a mortgage-backed security arbitrage, the point in time at which spread profits become great enough for the arbitrage to support itself, eliminating the gap interest rate exposure.

### Equivalent Bond Yield

A percentage used to express the comparison of the discount yield of money market securities with the coupon yield of government obligations.

### Equivalent Positions

Positions that have similar dollar-amount profit potentials but that are made up of differing securities. Equivalent positions have the same profit graph. For example, a covered call write is equivalent to an uncovered put write.

*See* Profit Graph.

### Escheat

State laws governing the disposition of abandoned property—particularly amounts of money, such as a bank balance. Although such assets usually revert to the state, their rightful owners can petition to claim the property later on.

### Escrow

Assets in a third-party account to ensure the completion of a contract by all parties.

### Escrow Payments

In a mortgage loan agreement, the amounts constituting ground rents, taxes, assessments, water rates, mortgage insurance premiums, fire and hazard insurance premiums, and other payments required to be escrowed by the mortgagor with the mortgagee.

### Escrow Receipt

Bank-issued receipt verifying that a customer (who has written a call) in fact owns the stock and that therefore the call may be considered covered.

### Eurocurrency (Euromoney)

The money that corporations or national governments deposit in banks away from their home countries, or *Eurobanks* (not necessarily banks in Europe). The *Eurodollar* is only one eurocurrency. There are also *Eurodollar bonds* and *Eurodollar certificates of deposit*, which are issued by banks outside the United States—primarily in Europe.

### European Currency Unit (ECU)

A "basket" of ten European currencies that serves as the currency for the European Monetary System. The unit's value is reassessed every five years or when the value has shifted 25% or more.

### Excess Reserves

The part of the total reserves of a bank that exceeds the statutory reserve requirement.

*See* Total Reserve.

### Exchange Distribution

The marketing of a large block of stock by one or two member organizations under special terms and conditions. Buy orders are solicited informally and then crossed with the large block of stock at the current market price on the floor of the exchange.

*See* Dist.

### Exchange-Type Company

An investment company created to take advantage of a specific individual tax ruling obtained by the investment company that enables an investor to swap "paper profits" on securities owned for shares in a more diversified investment company and still be able to defer payment of capital gains taxes on this exchange of assets.

### Ex-Clearing House

A term used to describe a transaction processed without benefit of clearing corporation facilities.

### Ex-Distribution

The security is trading so that the buyer will not be entitled to a distribution that is to be made to holders.

### Ex-Dividend (Without Dividend) Date

A date set by the Uniform Practice Committee or by the appropriate stock exchange, upon which a given stock will begin trading in the marketplace without the value of a pending dividend included in the contract price. It is closely related to and dependent on the date of record. It is often represented as "X" in the stock listing tables in the newspapers.

*See* Bond Interest Distribution.

### Execution

Synonym for a transaction or trade between a buyer and seller.

### Execution Report

A report that confirms the details of a trade and that is generated after a match is made (trader vs. contra side) and systematically routed to the originating branch.

### Executor/Executrix

A court-appointed person charged with the maintenance and distribution of the assets and liabilities of a deceased. Used when the deceased left a will.

### Exempted Securities

As defined in the 1934 Act, issues not subject to margin regulations, borrowing restrictions, registration requirements, proxy solicitations, and periodic statements of ownership. In general, these securities include any obligations of the U.S. government, as well as any obligations of its territories, possessions, states, or municipalities.

### Exempted Transactions

Transactions involving an exempted security.

### Exercise (Assign)

The requirement by an option holder for the seller of the option to perform the agreed-upon securities transaction. The seller (writer) of a call option must deliver (sell) stock to the option holder, whereas the seller (writer) of a put option must purchase it from the holder.

Exercises of index options are settled through the payment of cash. The cash settlement amount is the difference between the exercise price of the option and the current index value at the close of trading on the day of exercise, multiplied by the applicable index multiplier.

### Exercise Date

The date when the sale or purchase of an option takes place according to the contract.

### Exercise Limit

The limit on the number of contracts that a holder can exercise in a given period, as set by the appropriate option exchange. It is designed to prevent an investor or group of investors from *cornering* the market in a stock.

### Exercise Notice

A document delivered to the Options Clearing Corporation for listed options, or to the guarantor of a conventional option, legally requiring the writer of an option to perform his or her contracted obligations.

### Exercise of Call

The full or partial retirement of a bond issue through the use of a call privilege provided for in the terms of that security. The redemption price is usually higher than the face value if the option is exercised in the early years after the distribution.

The action of the owner of a call option when the option is exercised (when delivery of the underlying security is demanded).

### Exercise Price

*See* Strike (Striking) Price.

### Exim Bank

*See* Export-Import Bank.

### Ex-Legal

In municipals trading, the absence of a bond counsel's legal opinion usually connected with the delivery of the securities in the secondary market.

### Expected Return

The return an investor might expect on an investment if the same investment were made many times over an extended period. The return is found through the use of mathematical analysis.

### Expense Ratio

For a mutual fund, the expense ratio is the annual operating expenses (including management fees) divided by average annual net assets. In some cases, the management company may reimburse the mutual fund should the ratio exceed a certain percentage.

*See* Operating Ratio.

### Expiration Date

The date an option contract becomes void. The expiration date for listed stock options is the Saturday after the third Friday of the expiration month. All holders of options who wish to exercise must indicate their desire to do so by this date.

*See* Expiration Time.

### Expiration Time

The time of day on the expiration date when all exercise notices must be received. The expiration time is currently 5:00 PM on the business day preceding the expiration date. All times are Eastern Time.

*See* Expiration Date.

### Export-Import (Exim) Bank

Bank founded by Congress in 1934 to foster U.S. trade with other countries. The Eximbank borrows from the U.S. Treasury as an independent agent to fund its operations.

### Ex-Rights

A term applied to stocks trading in the marketplace for which the value of the subscription privilege has already been deducted and which therefore no longer bears such a right; it is literally trading "rights off."

### Extraordinary Item

In a report to shareholders, an unusual income or expense item not expected to occur again or to affect future years' operations.

### Extrinsic Value

The amount by which the market price of an option exceeds the amount that could be realized if the option were exercised and the underlying commodity liquidated. Also known as time value.

### Ex-Warrants

The security is trading so that the buyer will not be entitled to warrants that are to be distributed to holders.

### Face-Amount Certificate Company

An investment company that issues a debt instrument obligating itself to pay a stated sum of money (the face amount) on a date fixed more than twenty-four months after issuance, usually in return for deposits made by an investor in periodic installments.

### Face Value (Face)

The redemption value of a bond or preferred stock appearing on the face of the certificate, unless that value is otherwise specified by the issuing corporation. Also sometimes referred to as par value.

### Facilitation

The process by which a market is provided for a security. This usually refers to bids and offers made for large blocks of securities, such as those held by institutions. Listed options may offset part of the risk assumed by the trader who is facilitating the large block order.

*See* Hedge Ratio.

### Factor

The outstanding principal balance in a mortgage pool in decimal form. It represents the proportion of the original principal balance still outstanding.

### Factor Tape

A tape published twice monthly for each guarantor/program—that is, GNMA, FNMA, and FHLMC—which lists all pools issued in their respective markets and the current month's factor for each pool.

### Fail Contract (Fail)

A transaction between brokerage concerns that is not completed by delivery and payment on a settlement date.

*Fail Position*: The situation of the broker/dealer when after all the buy and sell transactions in a security have been netted out, owes another broker/dealer more securities than it has coming from still other firms.

*Fail to Deliver*: A situation in which the selling broker/dealer does not receive securities from the client in time to make delivery with the buying broker/dealer.

*Fail to Receive*: A situation in which the buying broker/dealer has not received the securities from the selling firm.

### Fair and Reasonable

*See* Five Percent Guideline.

### Fair Market Value

The price, based on the current market value determined by supply and demand, for which a buyer and seller are willing to make a transaction.

### Fair Treatment

Under the NASD Rules of Fair Practice, members have a business relationship with their customers and a fiduciary responsibility in handling their accounts.

### Fair Value

A term describing the worth of an option contract as determined by a mathematical model or used to indicate intrinsic value.

*See* Intrinsic Value; Model.

### Fannie Maes

*See* Federal National Mortgage Association.

### FANS

*See* Free Account Net Settlement.

### Farm Credit Banks

Banks set up to deal with the specific financial needs of farmers and their businesses.

### Farmers Home Administration (FHA)

Agency set up by the Federal Department of Agriculture empowered to make loans to farm owners or tenants to help finance the acquisition or improvement of farm properties. The FHA also helps finance community facilities by making loans to qualified municipal issuers.

### Farther Out, Farther In

The act of extending or retracting maturity or expiration dates on options.

### Fast Market

Term used to describe fast-paced activity in a class of listed options. If the exchange cannot control the market, new orders may be delayed.

### Fast-Pay Bonds

Bonds with high redemption priority over other bonds in an issue. They are redeemed at a faster rate than others in that issue.

### Federal Funds

The excess reserve balances of a member bank on deposit at a central bank in the Federal Reserve system. This money may be made available to eligible borrowers on a short-term basis.

Funds used for settlement of money market instruments and U.S. government securities transactions.

A term used to mean "same-day availability" of money.

*See* Clearing House Funds.

### Federal Funds Rate

A rate of interest associated with borrowing a member bank's excess reserves. The rate is determined by the forces of supply and demand.

### Federal Home Loan Banks (FHLB)

A government-sponsored agency that finances the home-building industry with mortgage loans from monies raised on offerings of bond issues; interest on these bonds is free from state and local income tax.

### Federal Home Loan Mortgage Corporation (FHLMC, Freddie Mac)

A private corporation authorized by Congress that sells participation certificates and collateralized mortgage obligations backed by pools of conventional mortgage loans. FHLMC is a secondary market facility of the Federal Home Loan Bank system. It sells participation sales certificates secured by pools of conventional mortgage loans whose principal and interest are guaranteed by the Federal Government. It also sold GNMA bonds to raise funds to finance the purchase of mortgages.

### Federal Housing Administration (FHA)

A private corporation and division of the Housing and Urban Development Department (HUD), authorized by Congress. Its main activity is insuring residential mortgage loans made by private lenders. It sets standards of construction and underwriting. FHA does not lend money or construct housing.

### Federal Intermediate Credit Banks (FICB)

An agency under the supervision of the Farm Credit Administration that makes loans to agricultural credit and production associations, with revenues derived from five-year bond issues. The interest on those bonds is free from state and local income tax.

### Federal Land Banks (FLB)

Government-sponsored corporations that arrange primary mortgages on farm properties for general agricultural purposes; interest on their bonds is exempt from state and municipal taxes.

### Federal National Mortgage Association (FNMA)

A publicly owned, government-sponsored corporation that purchases and sells mortgages insured by the Federal Housing Administration (FHA) or Farmers Home Administration (FHA); or guaranteed by the Veterans' Administration (VA). Interest on these bonds, called Fannie Maes, is fully taxable.

### Federal Open Market Committee

*See* Open Market Operations.

### Federal Reserve Bank

One of the banks forming the Federal Reserve system.

### Federal Reserve Board (FRB)

A United States government agency empowered by Congress to regulate credit in the country. Its members are appointed by the president of the United States.

### Federal Reserve Requirements

Each commercial bank must set aside a certain percentage of its deposits, as determined by the Federal Reserve, in order to limit its potential credit-granting capability.

### Federal Reserve System

A system of Federal Reserve banks in the United States forming 12 districts under the control of the Federal Reserve Board. These banks regulate the extension of credit as well as other banking activities.

### Fed Repo

Sale of securities by dealers to Federal Reserve, with understanding that Fed will sell them back at a specified time and price. The agreement can be broken by either party.

### FHA Experience

A statistical series, revised periodically, which represents the proportion of mortgages that "survive" a given number of years from their origination.

### FHLB

*See* Federal Home Loan Banks.

### FHLMC Participation Certificate

Certifies ownership interest in a specific pool of mortgages owned by FHLMC.

### FICB

*See* Federal Intermediate Credit Banks.

### Fidelity Bond Insurance

*See* Blanket (Fidelity) Bond Insurance.

### Fiduciary

A person or institution to whom property is entrusted for the benefit of another.

### FIFO

*See* First In/First Out.

### Figuration

In the back office of a brokerage firm, the calculations connected with a securities transaction. Performed in the Purchase and Sales Department, these calculations include sale price, margin, debit balance, commissions, and related charges.

### Fill-or-Kill (FOK) Order

An order that requires the immediate purchase or sale of a specified amount of stock, though not necessarily at one price. If the order cannot be filled immediately, it is automatically cancelled (killed).

### Final Money

*See* Net Price.

### Financial and Operational Combined Uniform Single (FOCUS) Report

A report required periodically of brokers by various regulatory authorities that gives vital statistics regarding the firm's capabilities to handle its business.

### Financial Principal

A registered principal of the NASD who is qualified to participate in the preparation and approval of a member firm's financial statement and net capital computations, besides all other phases of the business' operations.

*See* Principal Registration.

### Firm Market (Price, Quote)

In the OTC market, a quotation on a given security rendered by a market maker at which he or she stands ready and able to trade immediately.

### Firm Position

A firm's inventory position.

### Firm Yield Maintenance

Associated with a TBA trade, an FYM trade guarantees a specific yield to a customer instead of guaranteeing a specific coupon.

*Example:* 11% TBA at par may be settled by any coupon traded by GNMA during the TBA period. However, the price of the transaction would be changed to maintain an 11% yield.

### First In/First Out (FIFO)

A popular inventory cost accounting procedure in which the first item manufactured is assumed to be the first one sold by the company.

### First Section

Japan's largest stock exchanges—Tokyo, Osaka, Nagoya—are in two sections. First section stocks must meet strict listing requirements; after three years, they move on to the second section.

### Fiscal Policy

Actions taken by the federal government through the budgetary policy to shape and direct the economy.

*See* Monetary Policy.

### Five Percent Guideline

A general guideline established by the NASD Board of Governors to define "fair" in a random trading transaction; it is not a rule or regulation and is used only as a rough criterion for markups, markdowns, and commissions.

### Fixed Annuity

An annuity paying a fixed or predetermined amount of money periodically.

### Fixed Asset

An item of value used in current operations that would normally be of use for more than one year.

### Fixed Charge Coverage

The degree by which a corporation is able to earn its interest obligations from total income.

### Fixed Liability

An obligation of a corporation payable more than a year hence.

### Fixed Rate

An interest rate that does not vary with time or other conditions.

### Fixing Rate Option

The choice, usually available to a borrower, to change a floating or variable rate to a fixed rate for a period of one, two, three, six, and twelve months.

### Fixed Trust

A unit investment company that issues shares reflecting units in a packaged portfolio of securities, such as U.S. government or tax-exempt obligations.

### Flash Prices

When reporting falls six or more minutes behind activity on the stock exchange floor, transactions in 30 representative issues are periodically culled from their proper sequence and immediately published on the ticker tape.

### Flat

When accrued interest is not added to the contract price of bonds (that is, most income bonds and all obligations for which interest has been deferred) in a transaction, the bonds are said to be trading "flat."

### FLB

*See* Federal Land Banks.

### Flexible Payment Loan (FHLMC)

A note secured by a home mortgage, in which amortization of principal is not required during an initial period (that may not be greater than five years) of the mortgage loan term. During such period, the required payments must be great enough to pay the interest. The note must require repayment in monthly installments on a specified payment schedule, and, after the end of the initial period, the payments must retire the entire obligation, both interest and principal, within the remainder of the mortgage loan term (not to exceed 30 years, including the initial period). The coupon rate is not subject to increase during the initial period, except by agreement.

### Float

The number of shares issued and outstanding of a company's stock.

### Floating Rate

*See* Variable Rate.

### Floating Rate Mortgage

*See* Adjustable Rate Mortgage.

### Floor

The securities trading area of an exchange.

*See* Trading Post; Ring.

The lowest level of a floating (variable) rate, set by agreement.

*See* Capo.

### Floor Broker

A person who works on the exchange floor executing the orders of public customers or other investors who do not have physical access to the area.

### Flipper

Someone who buys stock and then sells it quickly. A flipper is considered a trader, not a long-term trader.

### Floor Brokerage

A fee paid to a broker on the floor for executing a trade.

### Floor Department

The department of the NYSE responsible for the administration and supervision of trading rules and regulations on the floor of the Exchange.

### Floor Order Tickets

Abbreviated forms of order tickets, used on the floor of the exchange for recording executions.

### Floor Trader

*See* Local; Registered (Floor) Trader.

### Flower Bond

A type of treasury bond selling at a discount with a special privilege attached permitting redemption after the death of the owner at par value in satisfaction of federal estate taxes. These bonds were issued prior to April 1, 1971, and will be in circulation up to final maturity in 1998.

### FMAN

*See* JAJO.

### FNMA

*See* Federal National Mortgage Association (FNMA).

### FOCUS

*See* Financial and Operational Combined Uniform Single (FOCUS) Report.

### FOK Order

*See* Fill-or-Kill (FOK) Order.

### Follow-Up Action

Any option trading that takes place after a position is established. It is generally used to limit losses or to take profits.

### Forbearance

When a creditor does not enforce a debt due.

### Form FR-1 (NASD)

*See* Blanket Certification Form.

### Formula Investing

Securities investments in the market using a fixed set of criteria.

### Forty-Eight-Hour Rule

The deadline for obtaining pool information assigned to a TBA contract. The seller must transmit this verbal information to the buyer no later than 3:00 P.M. EST of the second business day before the settlement date. If the information is not in time, the delivery date for the pool is moved forward one more day.

### Forward Contract

A contract in which one party guarantees to deliver a specified quantity of a commodity or financial instrument at a future date, in return for which the other party guarantees a set price. Such contracts are generally negotiated individually, unlike futures contracts, whose specifications are standardized. Forward contracts were used by commodity producers before the standardized futures contract, and they are still used internationally with the underlying financial instruments.

### Forward-Exchange Markets

The international currency market, in which companies may hedge their exchange rate risk.

### Forward Pricing

The means of determining purchase or redemption prices after receipt of a mutual fund order from a customer.

### Fourth Market

A term referring to the trading of securities between investors without the use of broker/dealers.

### Fractional Discretionary Order

An order to buy or sell at specified prices but with a fraction of a point leeway, to be exercised at the discretion of the broker if necessary.

*See* Discretionary Order.

### Franchise

*See* Seat (Franchise).

### FRB

*See* Federal Reserve Board.

### Free Account Net Settlement (FANS)

A securities depository organized and promoted by the NASD for use by its members in OTC transactions. Its purpose is to immobilize certificate movement and reduce opportunities for theft of these valuable documents.

### Free Box

A bank vault or other secure location used to store fully paid customer securities. The depositories of the NCC and DTC serve as free boxes for many member firm customers.

### "Free" Crowd

*See* Active Bonds (the "Free" Crowd).

### Free-Riding

As used in credit activities within the securities industry, the illegal practice of purchasing and selling an issue without showing ability and intent to pay for the transaction. The penalty for this practice is to freeze the account for 90 days.

### Free-Riding and Withholding

As defined by the NASD in distributions of hot issues, the failure of a member to make a bona fide offering of a security that the member is distributing as an underwriter or selling group member.

### Free Securities

A term used to describe securities unencumbered by a lien.

### Front-End (Prepaid Charge) Plan

A contractual investment plan in which most of the sales charges are applied to payments made in the early years.

### Frozen Account

A special cash account in which a customer sells a security he or she had purchased but not paid for, and then either (1) fails to pay by the seventh business day after the transaction, or (2) withdraws any portion of the proceeds before payment for the purchase. Full payment is required before any further purchase executions for 90 days.

### Full Disclosure Act

The Securities Act of 1933.

### Full Registration

A form of NYSE representative status that enables an employee to engage in the solicitation of all aspects of the securities business in which the firm participates.

### Full Trading Authorization

*See* Power of Attorney.

### Fully Diluted Earnings Per Share

A computation of earnings applicable to each share of common stock outstanding based on the supposition that all convertible securities were exchanged for common stock at the beginning of that accounting period.

### Fully Modified Pass-Through

A pass-through for which the timely payment of principal and interest is guaranteed by the issuer.

*Example*: A Ginny Mae.

### Fully Registered Bonds

Bonds registered as to both principal and interest.

### Funded Debt

The aggregate of a corporation's liabilities with maturities exceeding five years.

### Fundamental Analysis

A method for analyzing the prospects of a security through the observation of accepted accounting measures such as earnings, sales, assets, and so on.

*See* Technical Analysis.

## Funding Date (FHLMC)

The date on which Freddie Mac disburses payments to sellers for a mortgage purchased in whole or in part by Freddie Mac.

## Fungible

Interchangeable in law. The concept that one unit of a security is interchangeable with any other unit of the same security. For example, one share of AT&T common stock is interchangeable with any other share of AT&T common stock.

## Futures

Short for futures contract, which is an agreement to make or take delivery of a commodity at a specified future time and price. The contract is transferable and can therefore be traded like a security. Although futures contracts were once limited to commodities, they are now available on financial instruments, currencies, and indexes. Noncommodity futures contracts often differ from their predecessors in important respects; for example, "delivery" on an index is irrelevant.

### Gap

In technical analysis, a "break" between the trading ranges of a stock's price for two successive days. That is, the two ranges do not overlap. A gap usually signals a reversal because the market is overbought or oversold.

### Garage

One of the small trading areas just off the main trading floor of the New York Stock Exchange.

### Gather in the Stops

A tactic in stock trading in which enough stock is sold to drive its price down to a point where stop orders are known to exist. The stop orders become market orders, in turn creating movement and setting off more stop orders. This process is called *snowballing.*

### General Account

*See* Margin (General) Account.

### General Obligation (GO) Bond

A tax-exempt bond whose pledge is the issuer's good faith and full taxing power.

### General Partner

A member of a partnership whose participation, especially in liabilities, is unlimited. Such a member may have personal assets attached to satisfy a business-related liability.

### Gilt-Edged

A security (bonds more often than stocks) that consistently pays dividends or interest.

### Gilts

British and Irish government securities, as well as those of some local British authorities and overseas public sector offerings. In the secondary market, gilts may be traded on the London Stock Exchange.

### Ginnie Maes

*See* Government National Mortgage Association.

### Give Up

The practice by the payer of a commission or fee directing the recipient to "give up" part of the fee to another broker. In some situations the practice may be illegal.

### Glass-Steagall Act

The 1933 act that prohibits a financial institution from engaging in commercial activities (taking deposits, making loans) and investment banking (underwriting and trading securities) at the same time.

### GNMA

The GNMA security holder is protected by the full faith and credit of the U.S. government. The securities are backed by FHA, VA, or FMHA mortgages. The term "pass-throughs" is often used to describe Ginnie Maes.

When Congress partitioned FNMA into two corporate entities, GNMA took responsibility for the special assistance loan program and the management and liquidation functions of the older FNMA. GNMA also administers and guarantees mortgage-backed securities that channel new sources of funds into residential financing through the sale of privately issued mortgage-backed securities.

### GNMA Settlement

Usually the third Wednesday of the month, for all trades done since the last GNMA settlement.

### Go-Around

A process by which the Federal Open Market Committee gathers bids and offers from primary bank and nonbank dealers.

### Go-Go Fund

An investment company with a very speculative portfolio.

### Going Away

A term applied to the purchase of one or more serial maturities of an issue either by institution or by a dealer.

### Going Private

Moving a company's shares from public to private ownership, either through an outside private investor or by the repurchase of shares. A company usually decides to go private when its shares are selling way below book value.

### Going Public

A private company is "going public" when it first offers its shares to the investing public.

### Goldbug

Anyone preoccupied with gold as an investment, often because gold seems to provide "insurance" against worldwide economic disaster.

### Golden Handcuffs

A contract between a broker and a brokerage house, offering lucrative commissions, bonuses, and other benefits, as long as the broker stays with the firm. Upon leaving, the broker must return much of the compensation.

### Golden Parachute

Contract offered to top corporate executives providing extravagant benefits in case they lose their jobs in a takeover.

### Good Delivery

Proper delivery by a selling firm to the purchaser's office of certificates that are negotiable without additional documentation and that are in units acceptable under the Uniform Practice Code.

### Good Faith Deposit

An amount of money given by members of an underwriting syndicate to the syndicate manager to guarantee their financial performance under the syndicate agreement.

An amount of money deposited by a customer upon opening a new account.

### Good Money

Another term for federal funds.

### Good Name

A slang expression used to denote the registration of securities so as to permit good delivery (that is, not in legal form).

### Good-till-Cancelled (GTC or Open) Order

An order to buy or sell that remains valid until executed or cancelled by the customer.

*See* Limit; Stop; Stop Limit.

### Goodwill

The part of the value of a business that is based on good customer relations, high employee morale, and other factors.

### Government National Mortgage Association (GNMA)

An offshoot of the FNMA, a wholly owned government corporation (operated by the Department of Housing and Urban Development (HUD) that provides primary mortgages through bond issuances carrying no tax exemptions. GNMA securities, called "Ginnie Maes," are issued by mortgage bankers, S&L associations, savings banks, and other institutions.

### Graduated Payment Adjustable Rate Mortgage (GPARM)

Same as an ARM, except initial rate steps up in intervals, regardless of margin and index.

### Graduated Payment Mortgages (GPMS, Jeeps)

Mortgages issued by FHA, calling for graduations of payment in each of the first five years of a loan. The remaining period of the loan is at a set rate. GPMs are backed by GNMA.

Mortgages that differ from conventional mortgages because not all payments are equal. There is a graduation period where payments start at a relatively low level and rise for some number of years.

### Grantor Trusts

Trusts whereby the grantor (certificate holder) retains control over the income or assets, or both, to such an extent that the grantor is treated as the owner of the property (mortgage assets) and its income for tax purposes. The result is to make the income from a grantor trust taxable to the grantor but not to the trust receiving it.

### Graveyard Market

A bear market in which selling investors are faced with large losses, while prospective investors keep their money in cash until the market gets better.

### Greenmail

In response to a corporate takeover attempt, the "target" corporation buys back its shares from the potential acquirer at a premium. The would-be acquirer then abandons the takeover bid.

### Green Shoe

In an underwriting agreement, a clause that allows the syndicate to purchase additional shares at the same price as the original offering. This lessens the risk for the syndicate.

### Group of Five

The U.S., France, Japan, West Germany, and Britain. These countries, usually represented by their finance ministers or central bankers, meet several times a year to discuss economic issues.

### Group of Seven

The "enlarged" version of the Group of Five, including Canada and Italy.

### Group Sales

Sales of securities by a syndicate manager to institutional purchasers from "the pot."

## Growing Equity Mortgage (GEM)

A mortgage loan with an initial principal and interest payment sufficient to amortize the loan over its term. Each year the principal and interest payment is increased by a fixed percentage of the previous year's P&I payment. The interest rate remains constant throughout the term of the mortgage loan.

These mortgages are insured by FHA and are backed by GNMA; they have a maturity of 15 years instead of the standard 30 years.

## Growth Company (Stock):

A company (or its stock) that has made fast gains in earnings over the preceding few years and that is likely to keep on showing such signs of growth.

## Growth Fund

A mutual fund that invests in growth stocks, thereby providing long-term capital appreciation for shareholders.

## GTC

*See* Good-Till-Cancelled (GTC or Open) Order.

## Guaranteed Coupon (GTD)

In TBA trades, a specific coupon is guaranteed to a customer at the time a pool is assigned to a TBA. This is the converse of a firm yield maintenance (FYM).

## Guarantee Letter

A letter issued by a member of the Options Clearing Corporation to an options exchange guaranteeing the financial performance of a market maker.

## Guaranteed Account

An agreement whereby the equity of one account guarantees the financial integrity of another account.

## Guaranteed Annuity

*See* Fixed Annuity.

## Guaranteed Bonds

Bonds issued by a subsidiary corporation and guaranteed as to principal and/or interest by the parent corporation.

## Guaranteed Stock

Preferred stock whose dividend is guaranteed by someone other than the issuer.

## Gun Jumping

Illegally soliciting orders before an SEC registration is effective.

Buying a security based on information that is not yet public (that is, "inside information").

### Haircut

The amount taken off the value of securities for the purpose of computing a broker/dealer's net capital. The range of percentages taken off—the "haircuts"—runs for 0% for U.S. Government obligations to 100% for fail contracts.

### Half-Life

The period until half of the original principal amount of the pool is repaid.

*See* Duration and Average Life.

### Hammering the Market

The intensive sale of stocks to drive prices down.

### Hard Dollars

The dollars that a brokerage firm pays for analysis, research, or other client-related services.

### Head and Shoulders

In technical analysis, a bar chart pattern of a stock's price movement marked by a shoulder line, a neck line, and a head line resembling a person's upper torso. As the price moves toward the shoulder line, the analyst considers the trend bearish. This is known as a *head and shoulders top*. The reverse pattern, with the head at the bottom, is called a *head and shoulders bottom.* This pattern is considered bullish.

### Heavy Market

A market for a security or commodity that contains many more sellers than buyers. This market is characterized by falling prices.

### Hedge

Any combination of long and/or short positions taken in securities, options, or commodities in which one position tends to reduce the risk of the other.

### Hedge Clause

A statement that appears on a securities valuation, research report, or market letter in which the writer disclaims responsibility for inadvertent errors or omissions in the contents of the material.

### Hedge Fund

An investment partnership that aggressively buys securities of certain companies while selling short shares of other companies engaged in the same industry.

### Hedge Ratio

A mathematical quantity equal to the delta of an option. It is useful in facilitation because a theoretically riskless hedge can be established by taking offsetting positions in the underlying stock and its call options.

*See* Facilitation; Delta.

### Hemline Theory

Theory stating that the trend in stock prices goes hand-in-hand with the trend in the hemlines of women's dresses: If hemlines drop, so do stock prices.

### Highballing

The illegal act of swapping securities with a customer at price levels above that prevailing for those same issues under competitive conditions.

### Holder of Record

The party whose name appears on a company's stockholder register at the close of business on the record date. That party will receive a dividend or other distribution from the company in the near future.

## Hit the Bid

Term applied to the situation in which a seller accepts the buyer's highest bid. For example, if the as price is 34¼ and the bid 34, the seller "hits the bid" by accepting 34.

## Holding Company

An investment company formed to own a controlling interest in one or more subsidiary companies.

## Holding Period

The period that someone holds a capital asset.

## Holding the Market

Going into the market with enough buy orders to generate price support for a security. The purpose is to offset a downward trend. Viewed by the SEC as a form of illegal manipulation (except in the case of a new issue cleared by the SEC).

## Home Mortgage (FHLMC)

An instrument creating a valid first lien on real estate (held in fee simple or on an acceptable leasehold), on which there is located a structure or structures designed principally for residential use.

## Home Run

Any large gain by an investor in a short period, commonly the result of takeover bids.

## Horizontal Price Movement

In technical analysis, a string of transactions in which the prices change little. This pattern, if sustained, indicates no trend.

## Horizontal Spread

The term used to describe an options strategy where the options have the same striking price but different expiration dates.

*See* Calendar Spread.

## Hot Issue

A security that is expected to trade in the aftermarket at a premium over the public offering price.

*See* Withholding.

### Hot Stock

A security whose price rises quickly on the first day of sale.

Stolen stock.

### House

On the street, a firm or individual engaged in business as a broker/dealer or investment banker.

The London Stock Exchange.

### House Account

An account managed by a firm executive and/or handled at the firm's main office. No salesperson receives a commission or transactions in a house account.

### House Call

Notification of the customer by the brokerage house that the equity in a margin account is below the maintenance level.

### House Maintenance Requirements

The lowest level that a customer's margin account may decline before more equity must be supplied or all collateral will be liquidated.

### Housing Authority Bond

A municipal bond whose payment of interest and/or principal is contingent upon the collection of rents and other fees from users of a housing facility built with the proceeds of the issuance of the bond.

### $100 Rule

Same-day purchases and sales of different securities by the same customer that result in a cash deficiency of $100 or less do not mandate satisfaction under Regulation T.

### Hybrid Annuity

An annuity that is partly fixed and partly variable.

### Hypothecation

The act of borrowing money to finance purchasing or carrying securities while using those securities as collateral for the loan.

### Hypothecation Agreement

*See* Customer's Agreement.

### ID System

*See* National Institutional Delivery System.

### Immediate Family

Defined differently under various industry regulations. Generally, a husband or wife, children, grandchildren, grandparents, parents, in-laws, or any other relative in the same household.

### Immediate or Cancel (IOC) Order

An order that requires immediate execution at a specified price of all or part of a specified amount of stock: the unexecuted portion has to be cancelled by the broker.

### Implied Volatility

The volatility of the underlying stock, as determined by the price currently existing in the market at the time, rather than historical data on the price changes of the underlying stock.

*See* Volatility.

### Inactive Bonds

Debt instruments that are expected by the NYSE Floor Department to trade only infrequently. All bids and offers, therefore, are filed in a "cabinet" or "can" (on cards colored to reflect effective lifetimes) until they are cancelled or executed.

### Inactive Market

*See* Narrow Market.

### Income (Adjustment) Bonds

In the event of bankruptcy, long-term debt obligations are offered in exchange for outstanding bonds by the court-appointed receiver. The interest requirement associated with such debt will be paid by the corporation only when, as, and if earned.

### Income Companies

Investment companies that stress higher-than-average current income distributions without regard to quality or class of security in their portfolios.

### Income Shares (Stocks)

A class of securities issued by dual-purpose investment companies that entitles owners to net dividends and interest earned by the company's entire portfolio with a minimum amount guaranteed.

*See* Capital Stock.

### Income Statement

*See* Earnings Report.

### Incremental Return Concept

A strategy in covered call writing by which the investor strives to earn an additional return from option writing against a stock position targeted to sell at a substantially higher price.

### Indefinite Closure of Transfer Books

*See* Closure, Indefinite, of Transfer Books.

### Indenture

A written agreement between corporation and creditors containing the terms of a debt issue, such as rate of interest, means of payment, maturity date, terms of prior payment of principal, collateral, priorities of claims, trustee.

### Indenture Qualification Statement

For publicly offered debt instruments not subject to registration under the Securities Act of 1933 but subject to the Trust Indenture Act of 1939, the statement required to be filed with the SEC to comply with the latter act.

### Independent Agent (Broker)

*See* Two-Dollar Broker.

### Index

A stock market indicator, derived in the same way as an average, but from a broader sampling of securities.

### Index Fund

A mutual fund portfolio containing most of the securities in a broad-based index, such as Standard & Poor's or Moody's Index. The securities are present in the same proportion as they are included in the index. Its performance, according to the efficient market theory, should mirror the market as a whole.

### Index Options

Options on stock indexes.

### Indication

On the ticker tape, an approximation of the current quotes.

### Indication of Interest

An expression of consideration by an underwriter's circle of customers for investment in a new security expected to be offered soon. It is not a binding commitment on the customer or the underwriter.

### Indicator

A unit of measurement used by the securities market analyst to help forecast market direction, volume of trading, direction of interest rates, or buying and selling by corporations.

### Individual Identification

A system for segregating customer securities in accordance with SEC Rule 15c3-3 which requires that each stock certificate be specifically identified as belonging to a particular customer.

### Individual Proprietorship

*See* Proprietorship.

### Individual Retirement Account (IRA)

A qualified plan to provide retirement security for the individual created in 1974 by the Employee Retirement Income Security Act (ERISA). Rules were liberalized in 1981 to permit virtually all taxpayers who receive income to take advantages of the benefits of these plans.

### Industrial Development Bonds

Industrial revenue bonds issued to improve the environment and subject to certain Internal Revenue Service regulations with regard to the tax-exempt status of the interest payments.

### Industrial Revenue Bonds

Municipal bonds issued for the purpose of constructing facilities for profit-making corporations. The tax-exempt feature of these bonds may be restricted by certain Internal Revenue Service regulations. The corporation, rather than the municipality, is liable for the payment of interest and principal.

### Inflation

A general rise in prices.

### Initial Margin Requirement

The minimum equity requirement (in 1985, $2,000), as established by various Federal Reserve regulations and New York Stock Exchange Rules, at the time a security is purchased.

### Inside Market

The favorable, wholesale market price for a security available only to a market maker and other members of the NASD.

### Insider

An officer, director, or principal stockholder of a publicly owned corporation and members of their immediate families. This category may also include people who obtain nonpublic information about a company and use it for personal gain.

*See* Immediate Family.

### Installment Sale

A sale of securities whose proceeds are paid in installments with the contract price being set in advance. Concomitant gains or losses are prorated for tax purposes.

### Instinet

Acronym for Institutional Networks Corporation. Actually an automated execution service, it is registered with the SEC as a stock exchange. Subscribers, generally mutual funds and other institutional investors, search the system for contras without having to pay brokerage fees.

### Institution

A large organization engaged in investing in securities, such as a bank, insurance company, mutual fund, or pension fund. An *institutional broker* buys and sells securities for any of the above dealing in large volumes and charging a lower-than-usual per-unit commission. An *institutional investor* is any of the institutions above who buy and sell securities. An *institutional house* is any brokerage firm dealing with such institutions. *Institutional sales* are sales of any type of securities by such institutions.

### Institutional Delivery

*See* National Institutional Delivery System.

### Insubstantial Quantity

Under NASD interpretations regarding hot issues, 100 shares of stock or $5,000 face value in bonds is considered an "insubstantial quantity." It may be allocated to certain restricted parties.

### Intangible Asset

An item of value whose true worth is hard, or even impossible, to determine, such as goodwill, reputation, patents, and so on.

### Intercommodity Spread

A spread consisting of a long position and a short position in different but related commodities, in which the investor hopes to profit from the changing prices between commodities.

### Interdelivery Spread

A trading technique in futures or options whereby an investor buys one month of a contract and, in turn, sells another month in the same contract. The investor is hoping to profit from the price differences between the two months. For example, an investor buys a June wheat contract and simultaneously sells a September wheat contract for a higher price.

### Interest-Bearing

Term applied to any security paying face value at maturity plus interest at a specified rate and periodically over the life of the security.

### Interest Rate Futures

A futures contract on an interest rate. The contract calls for delivery of an instrument that will mature some time after the delivery date. It is based on the market's expectation of interest rates for the period in the contract.

### Interest Rate Option

An option on an interest rate. The option must be prepaid based on the interest rate. The grantor must receive higher premiums during higher interest rates to compensate for the higher cost of capital.

### Intermarket Spread

*See* Interdelivery Spread.

### Internal Rate of Return (IRR)

The rate at which future cash flows must be discounted in order to equal the cash cost of the investment.

### International Bank for Reconstruction and Development

An international bank (25% controlled by the United States) designed to loan monies to its members (approximately 90 countries) to develop and modernize industry.

### Interpolation

The calculation of a figure, using ratio techniques, that exists between two known figures.

### Interpositioning

An unethical and unfair practice by a broker/dealer of needlessly employing a third party between the customer and the best available market, so that the customer pays more on a purchase or receives less on a sale than he or she should.

### Inter-Vivos (Living) Trust

A legal instrument that appoints some person or institution to perform a specific function with a designated sum of money. The terms of this incumbency become effective during its creator's lifetime.

### In the Money

An expression used to denote a securities option with a strike price that is profitable in comparison with the current market value of the underlying stock—that is, an option with intrinsic value. A *call option* is considered in the money if the underlying stock is higher than the striking price of the call. A *put option* is considered in the money if the stock is below the striking price.

*See* Out of the Money; Intrinsic Value.

### In the Tank

Colloquial expression for a security or group of securities that is quickly losing value.

### Intracommodity Spread

A spread in which the trader buys and sells futures contracts in the same commodity, on the same exchange, but for differing months.

### Intraday

Meaning "within the day," this term is most often used to describe daily high and low prices of a security or commodity.

### Intrinsic Value

The immediate value of an option if it were to expire with the underlying stock at its current price, or the amount by which an option is in the money. For *call options,* it is the difference between the stock price and the striking price if that difference is a positive number. If the difference is not positive, it is considered zero. For *put options* it is the difference between the striking price and the stock price if the difference is positive, and zero otherwise.

*See* In the Money Time Value Premium; Parity.

### Inventory Turnover

A numerical indicator of the rapidity with which a corporation's inventory is manufactured and sold.

### Inverse Head and Shoulder

In technical analysis, a chart pattern resembling a person's upper torso turned upside down. Prices drop to a low and then return, drop again to a new low, return again, only to drop down to the first low and return still again.

*See* Head and Shoulders.

### Investment Advisor

A person, company, or institution registered with the SEC under the Investment Advisors Act of 1940 to manage the investments of third parties.

### Investment Advisors Act of 1940

A federal law requiring those who charge a fee for investment advice to register with the SEC. Exceptions include banks, some brokers, and newspapers with broad-based readership.

### Investment Banker

A broker/dealer organization that provides a service to industry through counsel, market making, and underwriting of securities.

### Investment Club

A group of investors who pool their money to invest jointly. What to do with the capital is decided by vote. These clubs enable investors with small amounts of money to participate in larger investments, teaching them, along the way, more about investing.

### Investment Company

An institution engaged primarily in the business of investing and trading in securities; includes only (1) face-amount certificate companies, (2) unit investment trust companies, and (3) management companies.

### Investment History

Under NASD interpretation with regard to a hot issue, certain customers must have made at least 10 purchases over a three-year period with an average dollar value equal to that of the hot issue allocated.

### Investment Letter

In a private placement of securities, a written agreement between a seller and buyer, stating that the buyer's intentions are for investment only and that he or she does not intend to reoffer the securities publicly.

### Investment "Skeleton"

A slang expression denoting a speculative security in a portfolio that failed to meet the investor's expectations or financial objective.

### Involuntary (Statutory) Underwriter

An individual or corporation that purchases an unregistered security and offers it in a public distribution without an effective registration statement. Such parties are subject to fine and/or imprisonment.

### IOC Order

*See* Immediate or Cancel (IOC) Order.

### IRA

*See* Individual Retirement Account.

### IRA Rollover

A tax law provision permitting a person who terminates employment and who receives a lump-sum distribution of pension benefits 60 days to reinvest that money in an IRA completely tax-free.

### Irredeemable bond

*See* Perpetual Bond.

A bond whose issuer does not have the right to redeem the bond before maturity.

### Irrevocable Trust

A trust that cannot be altered or terminated by its creator without the beneficiary's consent.

### Issue (Issuance)

Any of a company's class of securities.

The act of distributing securities.

### Issued-and-Outstanding Stocks

That portion of authorized stock distributed among investors by a corporation.

### Issue Date

The date on which an issuer places a security in the marketplace; it is the first day in which a debt instrument begins to accrue interest. In the case of guaranteed mortgage pass-through certificates backed by a pool, it is the first day of the month of issuance.

### Issue Date Principal Balance

In a mortgage pool, the principal balance of the mortgage note after crediting any appropriate deductions.

### Issuer

A corporation, trust, or governmental agency engaged in the distribution of its securities. Also known as "originator."

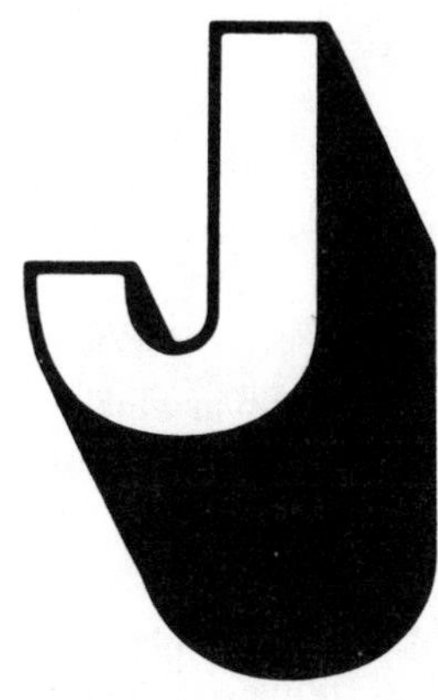

## JAJO

An abbreviation for January, April, July, October, the expiration months of option contracts. Most contracts usually have three to four months offered in a series at one time. Alternatives are *FMAN* and *MJSD*.

## Jeeps

*See* Graduated Payment Mortgages (GPM).

## Joint Account

An account including jointly two or more people.

## Joint Pool

A pool created when two or more FNMA-approved lenders participate under the same pool purchase contract.

## Joint Stock Company

A company with features of both a corporation and a partnership. Although the company is considered a corporation by law, the shareholders' liability is unlimited.

## Joint Tenants in Common

An account in which the two or more people participating have fractional interests in its assets. The interest percentage of the assets becomes part of each person's estate upon death.

### Joint Tenants With Rights of Survivorship (W/R/O/S)

An account in which two or more people have an ownership interest and whose assets are inherited by its survivors upon the death of any participant.

### Joint Venture

An arrangement whereby two or more people or firms work together on a project. Unlike a partnership, the joint venture is usually dissolved upon completion of the project.

### Junk Bond

Any bond with a Moody's or Standard & Poor's credit rating of BB or lower. Such bonds, usually issued by companies without long track records, can produce high yields.

### Keogh Plan

Initiated under the provisions of the Self-Employed Individuals Tax Retirement Act of 1962, this term applies to programs that enable an individual to defer payment of any income taxes on either a percentage of annual earned income or $30,000 until the individual retires and begins to withdraw funds from this accumulated pool of capital.

### Key Reversal Day

In technical analysis, the day on which a permanent reversal in the market takes place.

### Killer Bee

Colloquial term for anyone who helps a company avoid a takeover. Usually an investment banker makes the target look less attractive or harder to acquire.

### Know Your Customer Rule

*See* Rule 405.

### Kondratieff Wave

Soviet economist, Nikolai Kondratieff, devised this theory in the 1920s. He states that Western economies tend to go up and down in "supercycles" of 50 or

60 years. This controversial theory, he says, helped him to predict the economic crash of 1929–30.

### Krugerrand

One troy ounce of gold minted in coin form by the Republic of South Africa. It can sell for 4 or 5 percent more than its gold content or value.

### Lapsed Option

An option that expires unexercised.

### Last-In/First-Out (LIFO)

An inventory cost accounting procedure in which the last item manufactured is assumed to be the first one sold by the company. During an inflationary period, LIFO causes the cost of goods sold to be higher than if FIFO were used.

### Last Trading Day

Options cease trading at 3:00 PM Eastern Time on the third Friday of the expiration month.

### Late Tape

The exchange tape when it is very late in reporting completed transactions. When the tape falls behind five minutes or more, the first digit of transactions is deleted. For example, 47½ becomes 7½.

### Lay-Off

The sell-off by an issuer of any or all unsubscribed shares in a rights offering to the underwriters at the subscription price.

### Lead Manager

The member of an underwriting syndicate charged with the primary responsibility for conducting the affairs of the syndicate.

*See* Syndicate.

### Leg

A method of establishing a two-sided position involving a large amount of risk. The trader first executes one side of the position hoping to execute the other side at a later time and a better price. The risk materializes from the fact that a better price may never be available, and a worse price must eventually be accepted.

### Legal Delivery

A delivery of securities that is not good delivery because of the way in which registration of the certificates was carried out.

### Legal Investments (or Legals)

Securities investments deemed eligible for inclusion in portfolios of certain fiduciaries within the jurisdiction of the state departments. These investments are called "legal investments" or sometimes "legals."

*See* Legal List.

### Legal List

A list of securities published annually by some state banking and/or insurance departments that indicates items deemed suitable for investment by certain fiduciaries within the state's departments' jurisdiction. These investments are called "legal investments" or sometimes just "legals."

*See* Prudent Man Investment.

### Lending at a Premium

When securities cannot be obtained through the typical sources to cover a short sale, the short seller is obliged to pay lenders a fee for the use of their certificates in addition to the cash collateral normally provided. Lending at a premium usually brings a deluge of certificates into the market, thereby eliminating the need for the premium entirely.

*See* Lending at a Rate.

### Lending at a Rate

A situation in which short sellers, with their pick of lenders, demand interest for their cash collateral.

*See* Lending at a Premium.

### Letter Bonds

Privately sold bonds that are accompanied by an investment letter giving the investor the right to transfer or resell them.

### Letter of Guarantee

A letter from a bank to a brokerage firm guaranteeing that a customer who has written a call option does own the underlying stock and that the bank assumes delivery of the assigned call. The call can then be considered covered. Not all brokerage firms accept letters of guarantee.

### Letter of Indemnification

A letter required by most broker-dealers before acting on a seller's behalf for the sale of *shelf distribution* securities (securities that can be sold within two years of the effective date).

### Letter of Intent

A statement of intent by a mutual fund investor announcing his or her desire to invest over a period of thirteen months a large enough sum of money to qualify for a load discount.

*See* Breakpoint.

### Letter Security

An unregistered security offered privately in which the purchaser is obliged to sign an investment letter to complete the transaction and to forestall disciplinary action against the seller under the Securities Act of 1933.

### Level Debt Service

A requirement in a municipality's charter that the annual debt service payment must be approximately equal—or "level"—each year. Its purpose is to effectively budget all tax revenues of that municipality.

### Level Load Voluntary Accumulation Plan

A method of selling mutual fund shares by which sales commission per dollar of investment is the same throughout the plan and future investments may be stopped without penalty.

### Leverage

In securities, increasing return without increasing investment. Buying stock on margin is an example.

In finance, the relationship of a firm's debt to its equity, as expressed in the debt-to-equity ratio. If the company earns a return on the borrowed money greater than the cost of the debt, it is successfully applying the principle of leverage.

### Leveraged Buyout

Taking over a controlling interest in a company using mostly borrowed money.

### Leveraged Companies

*See* Dual Purpose (Leveraged) Companies.

### Leveraged Investment Company

An investment company that issues both income and capital shares. Income shareholders receive dividends and interest on investments, and holders of capital shares receive all capital gains on investment.

An open-ended investment company or mutual fund that may borrow capital from a bank or other lender.

### Leveraged Stock

Any stock bought with credit, such as in a margin account.

### Liabilities

All the outstanding claims against a corporation: accounts payable, wages and salaries, dividends declared payable, accrued taxes, fixed or long-term liabilities such as mortgage bonds, debentures, and bank loans.

*See* Assets; Balance Sheet; Equity.

### Liability Strip

A series of liabilities issued in varying maturities. Liability strips have composite yield costs and maturity measures.

### Life Tenancy

Ownership of a security for life that can be left to a beneficiary, as stated in a valid will.

### LIBOR

The current London Interbank Offering rate of interest.

### LIFO

*See* Last-In/First-Out.

### Limited Access to Books and Records

A shareholder's right to inspect financial information made public in accordance with federal, state, exchange, and NASD regulations.

### Limited Discretion

A term used in the maintenance of customer option accounts. Normally a customer gives a registered representative discretion in trading options limited to selling or exercising options that are in-the-money and about to expire.

### Limited Partner

A member of a partnership whose participation in liabilities and/or profits and losses has been limited by written agreement.

### Limited Partnership

A partnership with one or more limited partners.

### Limited Registration

A form of temporary NYSE representative status in which a firm employee is permitted to solicit business and service customers only in selected mutual funds and MIP accounts. This representative must qualify for full registration within seven months thereafter.

### Limited Trading Authorization

*See* Power of Attorney.

### Limit Order

An order in which a customer sets a maximum price he or she is willing to pay as a buyer and a minimum price he or she is willing to accept as a seller.

*See* Market Order; Stop Order.

### Limit Price

A modification of an order to buy or sell. With a *sell* limit order, the customer is instructing the broker to make the sale at or above the limit price. With a *buy* limit order, the customer is instructing the broker to make the purchase at or below the limit price.

### Liquidation

The voluntary or involuntary closing out of security positions.

### Liquidation Proceeds

Cash received (a) from the liquidation of defaulted mortgage loans, whether through the sale or assignment of the loans, trustee's sale, foreclosure sale or otherwise, or (b) from the sale of the mortgage property if the mortgage property is acquired in satisfaction of the mortgage.

## Liquidity

The ability of the market in a particular security to absorb a reasonable amount of trading at reasonable price changes. Liquidity is one of the most important characteristics of a good market.

The relative ease with which investors can convert their securities into cash.

## Liquidity Ratio

*See* Acid Test Ratio.

## Listed Bond Table

A daily publication appearing in many newspapers showing a summary of transactions by exchange or, if OTC, by security.

## Listed Stock

The stock of a company traded on a securities exchange and for which a listing application and registration statement have been filed with the SEC and the exchange itself.

## Listed (Stock) Option

A put or call option that is traded on a national option exchange and that is cleared through the Options Clearing Corporation. All listed stock options have fixed striking prices and expiration dates.

*See* Over-the-Counter Option.

## Listed Stock Table

A daily publication appearing in many newspapers showing a summary of transactions by exchange or, if OTC, by security.

## Living Trust

*See* Inter-Vivos (Living) Trust.

## Load

The portion of an offering price of shares in an open-end investment company that covers sales commissions and all other costs of distribution. The load is incurred only on purchases, there being, in most cases, no charge when the shares are sold (redeemed).

## Load Fund

A mutual fund whose shares are sold for a sales charge, or load. When investing in a load fund, the customer is advised by the salesperson when to sell or buy shares.

## Load Spread Option

The terms for allocating, or "spreading," the annual sales charge, or load, over a period of some years. For example, during the first four years of the contract, up to 20 percent of any year's contributions can be credited against the sales charge, but the total allocations for the four years may not exceed 64% of any annual contribution.

## Loan-to-Value (LTV)

The ratio, expressed as a percentage, of a mortgage loan amount divided by the value of the mortgaged property. For this calculation, *value* is the lower of the appraised value or the current purchase price of the mortgaged property. When the property is security for more than one mortgage the combined loan-to-value (CLTV) is the ratio, expressed as a percentage, of the total mortgage amounts, divided by the value of the mortgaged property.

## Loan Value

The maximum permissible credit extended on securities in a margin account, presently 50 percent of the current market value of eligible stock in the account.

## Local

In futures trading, a floor broker who buys and sells for his or her own account, seeking quick profits. A local may also execute orders for others.

## Locked Market

A highly competitive market in which the bids and prices are temporarily the same—that is, they are "locked."

## Lock-Up

A repo in which both securities and term are fixed prior to the transaction. Neither party can initiate terminations of the agreement.

## Lognormal Distribution

A form of statistical distribution most often applied to the movement of stock prices. It implies that stock prices can theoretically rise forever but cannot fall below zero.

### London Interbank Offering Rate (LIBOR)

A standard rate of interest used in international transactions.

### Long Market Value

The market value of securities owned by a customer (long in his or her account).

### Long Position

The ownership of securities.

### Long-Term Capital Transaction

A purchase with a subsequent sale more than six months later.

### Long-Term Debt

The debt of a company due and payable more than one year hence.

### Long-Term Gain/Loss

A profit/loss on an asset held longer than six months. A gain is eligible for preferential tax treatment. Special rules apply if the asset was a bequest or a gift.

### M

Abbreviation for 1,000. For example, "5M" means 5,000; "25M" means 25,000. Usually used to denote the face value of a bond.

Preceding the name of a stock in the National Quotation Bureau's daily pink sheet, the security can be margined.

### M 1

The nation's money supply, defined as total currency in circulation plus all demand deposits in commercial banks.

### M 2

M1 plus savings and time deposits of less than $100,000 in commercial banks.

### Maintenance Call

A broker/dealer's notice to a customer to deposit additional equity in his or her account to meet either New York Stock Exchange or the broker/dealer's own minimum maintenance requirements.

### Major Bracket Participant

A member of an underwriting syndicate who will handle a large part of the issue in relation to other members of the syndicate.

### Major Market Index

An index prepared by the American Stock Exchange and upon which futures contracts are traded.

### Maloney Act

Federal legislation passed in 1938 authorizing the registration of an association of securities broker/dealers with the SEC. The NASD and Municipal Securities Rulemaking Board are registered under this act.

### Managed Account

An account owned by one or more clients entrusted to a manager who decides when and where to invest it. Clients are charged a management fee for the maintenance of such accounts.

### Managed Fund

A fund actively managed according to investment policy and containing a portfolio of municipal securities.

### Management Company

An investment company that conducts its business in any manner other than as a face-amount certificate company or unit investment company.

*See* Closed-End Management Company; Diversified Management Company; Nondiversified Management Company; Open-End Management Company (Mutual Fund).

### Management Group

An organization that serves as an investment advisor to an open-end investment company.

### Mandatory Redemption Account

*See* Bond Amortization Fund.

### Manipulation

Making securities prices rise or fall artificially, through aggressive buying or selling by one investor or in connection with others. This is a severe violation of federal securities laws.

### Margin

The amount of money or securities that an investor must deposit with a broker to secure a loan from the broker. Brokers may lend money to investors for use in trading securities. To procure such a loan, an investor must deposit cash with the broker. (The amount is prescribed by the Federal Reserve System in Regulation T.) The cash represents the equity, or margin, in the investor's account.

*Example*: The "Reg T" requirement is 50%. An investor has $2,500 and wants to buy General Electric common stock, presently trading at 62⅜. The investor decides to desposit the $2,500 in an account with a broker as a Reg T requirement and borrow another $2,500 from the broker. With the total of $5,0000, the investor buys 80 shares of GE common ($5,000 divided by $62.375). The investor's equity, or margin, in the account represents the difference between the value of the stock (a liability) and the cash deposit (an asset): $5,000 – $2,500 = $2,500 margin.

In futures, the amount of money deposited with the broker to protect both the seller and the buyer against default. To establish a position in commodities, a client must deposit cash with the broker; the amount, or *rate of margin*, depends on exchange regulations and other factors. If a price change causes a contract to lose dollar value, the broker must require additional cash for the price variation; this is *variation margin*. If the client cannot meet the requirement, the broker may liquidate the contract, using the cash as necessary to offset the losses.

*Example*: The rate of margin is $1,000. The client deposits this amount of cash with the broker and buys a contract of soybeans (5,000 bushels). The market price drops 6 c/ a bushel, or $300 for the contract (5,000 bushels x 6 c/). The client's equity also drops $300 (from $1,000 to $700). The variation call is for $300 to restore the equity, or margin, to $1,000. Similarly, a market price rise will increase the amount of margin in the account.

*See* Hypothecation; Regulation T.

### Margin Agreement

*See* Customer's Agreement.

### Margin Call

A demand on the customer to deposit money or securities with the broker when a purchase is made or when the customer's equity in a margin account declines below a minimum standard set by an exchange or the firm.

### Margin (Credit) Department

A group within a securities firm that monitors all trade activites, ensuring that payment and delivery procedures are in accord with federal, exchange, and NASD regulations to which it is subject.

### Margin (General) Account

An account in which a customer uses credit from a broker/dealer to take security positions.

*See* Margin.

### Margin of Profit

Operating income divided by net sales.

### Margin Requirement

*See* Margin Call; Mimimum Maintenance Margin.

### Margin Security

According to Regulation T of the Federal Reserve Board, a margin security is (1) any stock, right, or warrant traded on one of the registered stock exchanges in the U.S.; (2) an OTC stock specifically declared eligible for credit by the Federal Reserve Board; (3) a debt security traded on one of the registered stock exchanges that either (a) is convertible into margin stock or (b) carries a right or warrant to subscribe to a margin stock. Investment company securities and any warrants to purchase a margin security are considered margin securities, whether traded on a registered stock exchange or not.

### Markdown

The fee charged by a broker/dealer acting as a dealer when he or she buys a security from a customer and sells it, at a higher price, to a market maker. The fee, or markdown, is included in the sale price and is not itemized separately in the confirmation.

*See* As Principal; Five Percent Guideline.

### Marketable Security

A security that may be readily purchased or sold.

A U.S. government bond freely traded in the open market.

*See* Certificate of Indebtedness (CI); Treasury Bills; Treasury Bonds; Treasury Notes.

### Marketability

How easily a security can be bought and sold.

*See* Liquidity.

### Market-If-Touched Order

An order allowable only on the CBOE. Such a buy order is activated when a series declines to a predetermined price or below. Such a sell order is activated when a series rises to a predetermined price or higher.

### Market Index

A general measurement of market movement, that, unlike an average, includes weighting of prices in terms of outstanding shares.

### Marketing Department

The Department of the New York Stock Exchange responsible for public relations.

### Market Letter

Sales literature published by a broker/dealer for customers focusing on factors that may affect securities prices.

### Market Maker

An options exchange member who trades for his or her own account and risk. This member is charged with the responsibility of trading so as to maintain a fair, orderly, and competitive market. He or she may not act as agent.

A firm actively making bids and offers in the OTC market.

### Market Not Held Order

An order to buy or sell securities at the current market with the investor leaving the exact timing of its execution up to the floor broker. If the floor broker is holding a "market not held" buy order and the price could decline, he or she may wait to buy when a better price becomes available. There is no guarantee for the investor that a "market not held" order will be filled.

### Market Order

An order to be executed immediately at the best available price.

### Market Price

The last reported sale price for an exchange-traded security.

For over-the-counter securities, a consensus among market makers.

### Market Servicer

A lender who coordinates the packaging of a joint pool and supervises the ongoing servicing activities of coservicers participating in the joining pool.

### Market Tone

The "health" of a market. The tone is good when dealers and market makers are actively trading on narrow spreads. It is poor when trading drops off and spreads widen.

### Market Value

The price that would be paid for a security or other asset.

## Marking

Manipulative action at the close by a trader during the execution of an option contract. The purpose of this action is to improve the equity position in the client's account, even if the transactions do not represent the fair value of the contract.

## Mark to the Market

As the market value of a borrowed security fluctuates, the lender may demand more in cash collateral for a rise in value, or the borrower may demand a partial refund of collateral for a decline. The written notice for either demand is a "mark" to the market.

## Markup

The fee charged by a broker/dealer acting as a dealer when he or she buys a security from a market maker and sells it to a customer at a higher price. The fee, or markup, is included in the sale price and is not itemized separately in the confirmation.

*See* As Principal; Five Percent Guideline.

## Married Put and Stock

If a put and stock are bought the same day and their position is designated a hedge, then they are considered to be "married."

## Matched and Lost

The results of flipping a coin by two securities brokers who are locked in competition to execute trades at the same price. The losing broker must tell the client that the demand or supply was not there in sufficient quantity as stipulated by the price.

## Matched Book

The accounts of securities dealers when their borrowing costs equal the interest earned on loans to customers.

## Matched Funding Arbitrage

An arbitrage established by purchasing an asset and selling a strip of liabilities that have similar maturity measures. Matched maturity measures can be established on the basis of average life, duration, or cash matching. The profit is realized as net interest spread.

## Matched Orders

Sales and purchases by the same beneficial owner of the same security at the same time and price, giving the impression of extensive trading in that security. This is a violation of the Securities Exchange Act of 1934.

### Matched Sale/Purchase Transaction (Reverse Repurchase Agreement)

A Federal Open Market Committee sale of Treasury bills or other government securities for cash settlement with a provision for repurchase at the same price plus interest on a specific date in the future.

### Matched Trade

A condition whereby both parties to a trade agree with the details of the transaction.

### Matrix Trading

A form of bond swapping in which traders take advantage of a temporary aberration in the yield spread differentials. These differentials may occur between bonds of the same class but with different ratings or between bonds of different classes.

### Maturity (Date)

The date on which a loan, bond, or debenture comes due; both principal and any accrued interest due must be paid.

### Maturity Value

The amount an investor receives when a security is redeemed at maturity; not including any periodic interest payments. This value usually equals the par value, although on zero coupon, compound interest, and multiplier bonds, the principal amount of the security at issuance plus the accumulated investment return on the security is included.

### MBSCC

*See* Mortgage-Backed Security Clearing Corporation.

### Member

A term used to describe a member of the New York Stock Exchange or other organized exchange or clearing corporation.

*See* Seat (Franchise).

### Member Bank

A bank that is a member of the Federal Reserve System. Member banks must purchase stock in the Federal Reserve Bank in their district equal to 6 percent of their own paid-in capital.

*See* Member Firm.

### Member (FHLMC)

Any Federal Home Loan Bank, the Federal Savings and Loan Insurance Corporation, or a financial institution which is a member of a Federal Home Loan Bank.

### Member Firm

A term used to describe a company that has as an officer or partner a member of the New York Stock Exchange, another organized exchange, or clearing corporation.

### Member Firms Surveillance Department

The department within the New York Stock Exchange responsible for the conduct of member firms.

### Member Takedown

A situation in which a syndicate member buys bonds at the takedown (or member's discount) and then sells them to a customer at the public offering price.

### Merger

The nonhostile and voluntary union of two corporations.

*See* Takeover.

### Message Switching

An automated communication procedure that links sales, operations, and trading locales by means of a computer. This electronic device routes orders, stores information, and relays execution reports to the proper departments and offices.

### Mezzanine Bracket

Colloquial name for underwriters who subscribe to the part of the issue not subscribed to by the major underwriters.

### Midgets

GNMA pass-through security with an intermediate term (15 years). It is similar in structure to the original 30-year GNMA security.

### Mill

Unit of measure equal to 1,000th of a dollar ($.001) or one-tenth of a cent.

### Minimum Maintenance Margin

The minimum equity customers must have in their accounts as defined by various Federal Reserve regulations and New York Stock Exchange rules. In 1985, for example, 25% of long market value must equal equity.

### Minimum Trading Variation

The minimum amount of variation allowable in the trading values in an exchange, usually one-eighth of a point.

*See* Point.

### Minus Tick

A transaction on an exchange at a price below the previous transaction in a given security.

### MIP

Acronym for Monthly Investment Program (Plan).

### Missing the Market

The failure by a member of the exchange to execute an order due to his or her negligence. The member is obliged to promptly reimburse the customer for any losses due to the mistake.

### Mixed Account

A margin account containing both long and short positions in securities.

### MJSD

*See* JAJO.

### Mobile Home (MH) Pass-Through

These mortgages are secured by mobile homes or by "combination" mobile home units and development lots. MHs are backed by GNMA.

### Model

A formula used to price an option as a function of certain variables such as stock price, striking price, time to expiration, volatility, dividends to be paid, and the current risk-free interest rate.

### Monetary Policy

The actions of the Federal Reserve System to affect the money supply, banking system, and, ultimately, the economy as a whole.

*See also* Fiscal Policy.

### Monetary Supply

*See* M1; M2.

### Money

Coin or certificates generally accepted in payment of debts for goods and services.

### Money Market

The market for dealers who trade riskless, short-term securities: T-bills, certificates of deposits, banker's acceptances, and commercial paper.

### Money Market Fund

Name for an open-ended investment company whose portfolio consists of money market securities.

### Money Market Instruments

Short-term debt (of less than one year to maturity) usually issued at a discount and not bearing interest. For example, Treasury bills, commercial paper, or banker's acceptances.

### Money Partner

The individual or organization in a joint venture providing the funds for enterprise.

### Money Supply

*See* Ml; M2.

### Monthly Payment

The scheduled monthly payment of principal or interest on a mortgage loan.

### Monthly Remittance

The total of the interest and principal distribution amounts remitted to mortgage-backed security holders on each remittance date.

### Moody's Investors Service

One of the best-known bond rating agencies, owned by Dun & Bradstreet. *Moody's Investment Grade* assigns letter grades to bonds based on their predicted long-term yield (MIGl, MIG2, etc). Moody's also rates commercial paper, municipal short-term issues, and preferred and common stocks. Another publication is a six-volume annual, with weekly or semiweekly supplements, giving great detail on issuers and securities. Publications include *Moody's*

*Bond Record* and *Moody's Bond Survey*. Moody's investment ratings are considered the norm for investment decisions by fiduciaries.

### Moral Suasion

An expression used to denote the Federal Reserve Board's ability to influence member bank financial policies by threatening to employ drastic powers in order to gain compliance with its own preferences.

### Mortgage (Loan)

A temporary and conditional pledge of property as security against a debt (loan).

### Mortgage-Backed Bond

A bond whose payments are secured by a set of mortgages.

### Mortgage-Backed Certificate (Security)

A security (1) that is issued by the Federal Home Loan Mortgage Corporation, the Federal National Mortgage Association, and the Government National Mortgage Association, and (2) that is backed by mortgages. Payments to investors are received out of the interest and principal of the underlying mortgages.

### Mortgage-Backed Security (MBS)

A security backed by loans on real estate property issued by mortgage bankers, commercial banks, savings banks, and other institutions. The majority of these issues are backed by the full faith and credit of the U.S. government. They serve as a conveyance of interest in real property given as security for the payment of a debt.

In some states, a deed of trust.

### Mortgage-Backed Security Clearing Corporation (MBSCC)

Established in 1979 by the Midwest Stock Exchange, Inc., to standardize and reduce the cost and potential risk associated with post-mortgage-backed securities trading activities. The MBSCC provides centralized trade comparison, margin consolidation, and settlement services for dealers, brokers, mortgage bankers, commercial banks and thrift institutions active in the GNMA and FHLMC forward markets.

### Mortgage Banker

A company that specializes in originating mortgage loans for sale to investors. It frequently continues to service the loans it has sold. As the local representative or regional or national institutional lenders, it acts as a correspondent between lenders or borrowers.

These mortgage loans are secured by real property to be pooled for backing issues of mortgage-backed securities. These pools are sold to an investor, with servicing retained for the life of the loan.

### Mortgage Bond

The most prevalent type of secured corporate bond. The bondholders are protected by the pledge of the corporation's real assets evaluated at the time of issuance.

*See* Closed-End Provision; Open-End Provision; Prior Lien Bond.

### Mortgagee

The institution, group, or person to whom property is conveyed as collateral for a loan made by the creditor.

### Mortgage Pool

A group, or "pool," of mortgages on the same class of property, with the same interest rate and the same maturity date.

### Mortgage REIT

A REIT primarily engaged in the financing of new construction.

### Mortgagor (Mortgager)

A person who mortgages property.

The obligor on a mortgage note.

### Mortgage Yield

An industry convention. For most securities, an internal rate of return calculation based on a 12-year life assumption.

### Moving Average

The average of security or commodity prices over a period of a few days or up to several years showing the trends for the last interval. Each time the average is taken, the oldest price is dropped and the latest price is added. Thus the average is a "moving" one.

### MSRB

*See* Municipal Securities Rulemaking Board.

## Multiple Pool

A pool consisting of mortgages purchased from more than one lender.

## Multiplier Effect

The leveraged power of loan expansion enjoyed by commercial banks using reserve balances as a base requirement.

*See* Velocity.

## Municipal Bond (Security)

Issued by a state or local government, a debt obligation whose funds either may support a government's general financing needs or may be spent on special projects. Municipal bonds are free from federal tax on the accrued interest and also free from state and local taxes if issued in the state of residence.

## Municipal Securities Rulemaking Board (MSRB)

Registered under the Maloney Act in 1975, the Board consists of industry and public representatives. It is designed to create rules and regulations for municipal bond trading among brokers, dealers, and banks. Its powers are similar to those of the NASD.

## Munifacts

A private communications network originating in the New York offices of *The Bond Buyer.* It transmits current bond market information to subscribers.

## Murphy's Law

The theory that if there's a wrong way to do something, someone will find it.

Gordon's Variation: If something is designed to be foolproof, someone will design a better fool.

If something can go wrong, it will go wrong, at the worst possible moment.

## Mutilation

A term used to describe the physical condition of a certificate, note, bond, or coupon when the instrument is no longer considered negotiable. The standards for determining what is considered mutilated are set forth in MSRB Rule G-12(e) (ix). Such missing items as the signature of the authorized officer, the serial number of the instrument, the amount or the payable date would cause the instrument to be considered mutilated. The issuing authority, or its agent, must be contacted to obtain certain documents needed to make the instrument negotiable again.

## Mutual Fund Company

*See* No-Load Mutual Fund; Open-End Management Company (Mutual Fund); Plan Company.

## Mutual Fund Custodian

A commercial bank or trust company with certain qualifications that holds in safekeeping monies and securities owned by an open-end investment company and accumulation plans of its shareholders.

### N

"Note" when used in lowercase with a U.S. government bid-asked quotation.

"Newly listed" when used in lowercase with a stock transaction report in the newspaper.

"New York Stock Exchange" when used as a capital next to a stock transaction report.

### Naked Option

An option that is written without any corresponding security or option position as protection in seller's account.

### Narrowing the Spread

The action taken by a broker/dealer to narrow the spread between bids and offers, by bidding higher or offering lower than the previous bid or offer. Also called closing the market.

### Narrow Market

Light trading and great price fluctuations with regard to the volume on a securities or commodities market. Also known as thin market and inactive market.

### NASD

*See* National Association of Securities Dealers.

### NASDAQ

*See* National Association of Securities Dealers Automated Quotations.

### NASDAQ OTC Price Index

*See* National Association of Securities Dealers Automated Quotations Over-the-Counter Price Index.

### NASD Code of Arbitration

Code governing the arbitration of controversies arising out of, and relating exclusively to, securities transactions. This code is available for disputes between members of the National Association of Securities Dealers or between customers and NASD members.

### NASD Code of Procedure

Code prescribed by the Board of Governors of the National Association of Securities Dealers for the administration of disciplinary proceedings stemming from infractions of the Rules of Fair Practice.

### NASD Form FR-1

A form required of foreign securities dealers by the Naational Association of Securities Dealers. By signing this form, dealers agree to abide by the NASD Rules of Fair Practice concerning a hot issue.

### National Association of Securities Dealers (NASD)

An association of broker/dealers in over-the-counter securities organized on a nonprofit, non-stock-issuing basis. Its general aim is to protect investors in the OTC market.

### National Association of Securities Dealers Automated Quotation System (NASDAQ)

A computerized quotations network by which NASD members can communicate bids and offers.

*Level 1* Provides only the arithmetic mean of the bids and offers entered by members.

*Level 2* Provides the individual bids and offers next to the name of the member entering the information.

*Level 3* Available to NASD members only, enables the member to enter bids and offers and receive Level 2 service.

### National Association of Securities Dealers Automated Quotations Over-The-Counter Price Index

A computer-oriented, broad-based indicator of activity in the unlisted securities market, updated every five minutes.

### National Clearing Corporation (NCC)

An NASD affiliate organization responsible for arranging a daily clearance of transactions for members by means of a continuous net settlement process. Although its principal office is in New York City, it operates electronic satellite branches in major U.S. cities.

### National Institutional Delivery System (NIDS)

A system of automated transmissions of confirmation from a dealer to an institutional investor, and the affirmation and book-entry settlement of the transaction. MSRB rules state that NIDS must be used on certain transactions between dealers and customers. Also known as "Institutional Delivery," or ID for short.

### National Market Advisory Board

Mandated by the Securities Act of 1975, the board is responsible for advising the SEC regarding the operations and regulations of the nation's security markets. The board is comprised of 15 members, serving terms of between two and five years, with a majority coming from the securities industry.

### National Quotation Bureau, Inc. (NQB)

A subsidiary of Commerce Clearing House, Inc. that distributes to subscribers several lists a day of broker/dealers making bids and/or offerings of securities traded over-the-counter. Also known as pink sheets.

### National Quotations Committee

A national committee of NASD that sets minimum standards for the publication of quotations furnished to newspapers, radio, or television.

### National Securities Clearing Corporation

A corporation organized to consolidate clearing securities nationally regardless of where the trade occurred. Designed to, among other things, consolidate SIAC and NCC.

### Natural

*See* Clean.

### NAV

*See* Net Asset Value (NAV) per Share.

### NCC

*See* National Clearing Corporation.

### Near Money

A bond whose redemption date is near.

Any asset that easily converts into cash, such as government securities, time deposits, or money market funds.

### Negotiability

In reference to securities, the ability to easily transfer title upon delivery.

### Negotiable Order of Withdrawal

A negotiable withdrawal ticket from a bank or savings and loan account.

### Negotiable Paper or Instrument

An order or promise to pay an amount of money that is easily transferable from one person to another, such as a check, promissory note, or draft.

### Negotiated Bid

A bid on an underwriting that is negotiated by the issuer and a single underwriting syndicate.

*See* Competitive Bid.

### Negotiated Marketplace

The over-the-counter market, in which transactions are negotiated between two parties. The opposite of auction marketplace.

### Negotiated Underwriting

The underwriting of new securities issues in which the spread purchase price and the public offering price are determined through negotiation rather than through bidding.

*See* Negotiated Bid.

### Net

*See* Netting.

### Net Asset Value (NAV) per Share

Net assets divided by the number of outstanding shares.

For an open-end investment company, often the net redemption price per share.

For a no-load, open-end investment company, both the net redemption price per share and the offering price per share.

### Net Change

The last column in a listed stock or bond table showing the difference between the closing prices of that day and the last day of the security traded, adjusted for dividends and other distributions.

*See* Listed Bond Table; Listed Stock Table.

### Net Earnings

*See* Net Income.

### Net Income

The income of a company after deducting all expenses from all revenues. Also called net earnings.

### Net Interest Cost

The net cost to the issuer of a debt instrument, taking into account both the coupon and the discount or premium on the issue.

### Net Interest Margin

The annual net spread between assets and the total of liabilities and retained profits, calculated using pro forma income results. The measure is analogous to return on total capital.

### Net Liquid Assets

Loosely defined as the excess of cash, readily marketable securities, and accounts receivable over all liabilities.

*See* Acid Test Ratio.

### Net Order

*See* Contingent Order.

### Net Price (Net Proceeds)

The proceeds of a sale or the gross payment on a purchase after deducting or adding, respectively, all expenses. Also known as "final money."

The contract price less all expenses incurred on a sale execution.

*See* Net Price.

### Net Profit Margin

The ratio of net profit divided by net sales.

### Net Quick Assets

Quick assets minus all current liabilities.

### Net Sales

Gross revenues realized less discounts, refunds, and returns of merchandise.

### Net Tangible Asset Value per Share (Book Value)

All tangible assets of a corporation minus total liabilities, divided by the total number of shares outstanding. For a mutual fund, it is portfolio value plus all other assets minus management group fees and all other liabilities, divided by the number of outstanding fund shares.

### Netting

An automated clearing process whereby sequences of transactions in a single issue of securities are consolidated and then reduced into a small number of delivery obligations. The CNS (Continuous Net Settlement) system allows the netting of transactions for a given settlement date against all open positions from prior settlement dates, as well as the automated transmission of instructions for the book-entry delivery.

### Net Working Capital

The excess of current assets over current liabilities.

*See* Working Capital.

### Net Worth

*See* Shareholders' Equity.

### Net Yield

On a mortgage-backed security, gross coupon less servicing spread—the yield to delivered to the customer.

### Neutral

A term used to describe an option that is neither bearish nor bullish. Neutral option strategies perform best if there is little or no net change in the price of the underlying stock.

*See* Bearish; Bullish.

### New Account Report

A mandatory document for broker/dealers who conduct a customer business, this is a record of inquiry probing into the essential facts relative to the background, financial circumstances, and investment objectives of each customer.

### New Issue

Any authorized but previously unissued security offered for sale by an issuer.

The resale of treasury shares.

### New Money

The issue of new bonds with a greater par value than that of bonds being called or maturing.

### New Money Preferred

Preferred stocks issued after October 1, 1942 providing corporate holders with an 85-percent tax exclusion on cash dividends. Preferred shares issued before this date enjoyed only a 60-percent exclusion.

### New York Plan

A method of issuing equipment trust certificates (serial debt obligations issued by airlines, railroads, and other common carriers) to acquire equipment.

*See* Philadelphia Plan.

### New York Stock Exchange Gratuity Fund

A fund created to provide $20,000 death benefits to the next of kin of each deceased member of means of voluntary contributions; coverage is limited to NYSE members exclusively.

### New York Stock Exchange Index

A "weighted" market index consisting of all common stocks listed on the Big Board, further broken down into (1) industrial, (2) transportation, (3) utilities, and (4) finance. The index is updated and printed every half hour on the "ticker tape" (actually an electronic screen).

### New York Times Market Indicators

A report in that newspaper of vital statistics regarding the previous day's stock market conditions.

### Next-Day Contract

A security transaction calling for settlement the day after trade date.

### NH

*See* Not Held (NH) Order.

### NIDS

*See* National Institutional Delivery System.

### Nifty-Fifty

The 50 stocks most favored by institutional investors.

### Nine Bond Rule

Unless prior consent of the NYSE can be obtained, all orders for nine listed bonds or fewer must be sent to the floor for a diligent attempt at execution.

### NL

*See* No-Load Mutual Funds.

### No-Action Letter

In response to a query as to whether an activity is in violation of securities regulations, the SEC may issue a letter stating that it will take no action, criminal or civil, if the activity is not in violation.

### No-Load Mutual Funds

Mutual funds offered directly to the public at net asset value with no sales charge.

### Nominal Exercise Rate

In a GNMA option, the dollar value determined by multiplying the strike price times the unpaid principal balance on the certificate with an 8-percent stated rate of interest.

### Nominal Quotation

A quotation that is an approximation of the price that could be expected on a purchase or sale, and that is not to be considered firm in the event that a purchase or sale is consummated.

*See* Numbers Only.

### Nominal Value

*See* Face Value; Par Value.

### Nominal Yield

The annual interest rate payable on a bond, specified in the indenture and printed on the face of the certificate itself. Also known as coupon yield.

### Nominee Name

A certificate registration in the name of a partnership acting in a fiduciary capacity. This form of registration is useful to facilitate delivery of certificates that would otherwise require supporting documentation.

### Nonmember (FHLMC)

A mortgage lender, not an FHLMC member, which has been approved by Freddie Mac as an eligible seller.

### No-Par Value

Stock with no dollar value assigned on the issuance of certificates but with an arbitrary equity interest assigned for use in preparing financial statements.

### Nonclearing Member

A member firm of the NYSE whose clearing operations are not handled by the Stock Clearing Corporation.

### Noncumulative Preferred Stock

Preferred stock on which omitted dividends do not accrue and the shareholders have no claim to them in the future.

### Nondiversified Management Company

Any management company that declares itself not subject to the limitations defining a diversified management company.

### Nonpurpose Loan

A loan involving securities as collateral that is arranged for any purpose other than to purchase, carry, or trade margin securities.

*See* Purpose Loans.

### Nonrecourse Loan

With respect to a direct participation program, a limited partner can borrow money, securing it by what he or she owns in the venture. If the borrower defaults, the lender has no recourse to the partnership's assets beyond those on which the money was borrowed.

### Nonrecurring Item

*See* Extraordinary Item.

### Normal Investment Practices

As defined by the NASD Board of Governors, the history of investment practices between the member firm and its customer. For customers subject to the NASD definition of restricted categories, no new accounts may be opened with the broker/dealer to purchase a hot issue. For customers not so restricted, the customer's investment objectives and financial circumstances must be considered.

### Normal Market

In futures trading, a market with adequate supply. In this type of market, the price of a commodity for future delivery should be equal to the present cash price plus the amount of carrying charges needed to carry the commodity to the delivery date.

### Normal Trading Unit

The accepted unit of trading in a given marketplace: On the NYSE it is 100 shares (round lot) for stocks and $1,000 par value for bonds. In some relatively inactive stocks, the unit is 10 shares. For NASDAQ traded securities it is 100 shares for stocks and $10,000 par value for bonds.

*See* Odd Lots; Round Lots.

### Normal Yield Curve

A graph that plots the yield of equivalent securities with different maturities at any given point in time. A *normal yield curve* indicates that short-term securities have lower interest rates than long-term securities.

### Note

A debenture generally with a maturity of one to five years.

### Not Held (NH) Order

An order that does not hold the executing member financially responsible for using his or her personal judgment in the execution price or time of a transaction.

*See* Market Not Held Order.

### Notice of Redemption

The announcement of an issuer's intention to call bonds prior to their dates of maturity.

### NQB

*See* National Quotation Bureau, Inc.

### NSCC

*See* National Security Clearing Corporation.

### Numbers Only

A dealer's response to a request for a quote with just numbers; the dealer is not obligated to make a transaction.

*See* Nominal Quotation.

### NYSE Stock Transfer Rules

A document set down by the Board of Directors of the New York Stock Exchange listing all the exchange rules concerning the who, what, why, when, where, and how of legal stock transfer.

### OBO

*See* Order Book Official.

### OCC

*See* Options Clearing Corporation.

### Odd Lot

An amount of stock less than the normal trading unit. *See* Round Lot.

### Odd-Lot Differential

Generally, the dealer who facilitates an odd-lot transaction will *buy* the securities ⅛ or ¼ point below the next round-lot trade, or *sell* the securities ⅛ or ¼ above the next round-lot trade.

### Odd-Lot Theory

A theory of market activity stating that small (odd-lot) investors frequently become heavy buyers as the market peaks and that they sell heavily in a declining market, just prior to a rally.

### Off-Board

An expression that may refer to transactions over the counter in unlisted securities or to transactions involving listed shares that were not executed on a national securities exchange.

### OECD

*See* Organization for Economic Cooperation and Development.

### Offer

The price at which a person is ready to sell.

*See* Bid-and-Asked Quotation (or Quote).

### Offering (Asked) Price

The lowest price available for a round lot.

### Offering Circular

A publication that is prepared by the underwriters and that discloses basic information about an issue of securities to be offered in the primary market.

Sometimes used to describe a document used by dealers when selling large blocks of stock in the secondary market.

### Offering Scale

The price, expressed in eights of a point or in decimals, at which the underwriter will sell the individual serial maturities of a bond issue.

### Offer Wanted (OW)

Notation made, usually in the pink or yellow sheets, by a broker/dealer who wants another dealer to make an offer for a security.

### Off-Floor Order

An order that originates off the floor of the NYSE and that has priority over on-floor orders.

### Office of Supervisory Jurisdiction (OSJ)

An office set up by individual member firms in compliance with Section 27 of the NASD Rules of Fair Practice. The office is managed by a registered principal who reviews a firm's supervisory responsibilities.

### Office Order Tickets

Transaction order forms filled out in great detail at each sales office of member firms.

*See* Floor Order Tickets.

### Official Notice of Sale

An advertisement issued by a municipal issuer to solicit competitive bids for an upcoming municipal bond issue. It usually includes all the facts about the issue and appears in the *Daily Bond Buyer*.

### One-Cancels-the-Other Order

Two or more orders to be treated as a unit. If one order is executed, the other is canceled.

### On-Floor Order

An order originating on the floor of the exchange.

### On-the-Quotation Odd-Lot Order

An odd-lot order that must be executed immediately; the price is therefore based on the existing round-lot quotation on the floor of the New York Stock Exchange or on some other exchange.

### On the Tape

A trade reported on one of several ticker tapes.

### OPD

Appearing next to a ticker symbol, these letters indicate an issue's initial transaction during a trading session if the price is significantly different from the previous day's closing transaction or the ticker price of the transaction did not get published shortly after execution.

### Open Box

*See* Active Box.

### Open-End Management Company (Mutual Fund)

A management company that offers shares (mutual funds) continuously after an initial offering, thereby altering its capitalization from day to day.

### Open-Ended (Open-End)

An agreement that has no fixed limits as to time, considerations, or interest. An open-end mortgage, for example, permits additional sums to be borrowed against the same security.

### Open-End Provision

A mortgage bond provision that enables a corporation to use the same real assets as collateral for more than one bond issue. In the event of default, creditors of all issues have equal claims.

## Opening

The price at which a security or commodity starts trading.

A short period during which interest rates drop and corporations can issue bonds at reduced prices.

## Opening Only Order

*See* At-the-Opening (Opening Only) Order.

## Opening Transaction

Any trade that increases an investor's position.

*Purchase*: An opening purchase transaction, so as to establish a new long position, adds long securities to the account.

*Sale:* The writing or selling of a listed option, so as to establish a new short position, adds short securities to the investor's net position.

*See* Closing Transaction.

## Open Interest

The total number of outstanding option or commodity contracts issued by the responsible clearing corporations.

## Open Market Operations

The activity of the Federal Open Market Committee, in behalf of the Federal Reserve Banking System, to arrange outright purchases and sales of government and agency securities, matched sale/purchase agreements, and repurchase agreements in order to promote the monetary policy of the Federal Reserve Board.

## Open on the Print

Term used when a block positioner takes the contra side of the trade from an institution. The transaction is printed on the tape, but buyers and sellers are still needed to offset the risk.

## Open Order

*See* Good-till-Cancelled (GTC or Open) Order.

## Open Outcry

On a commodity exchange, the shouting out of orders to trade. A trader shouts a selling price and a buyer shouts a purchase price. When the two are the same, the contract is recorded.

### Operating Income

Net sales less cost of sales, selling expenses, administrative expenses, and depreciation. The pre-tax income from normal operations.

### Operating Ratio

A comparison of operating expenses to net sales.

### Operations Department

A department of the NYSE responsible for (1) the listing and delisting of corporate and government securities, and (2) all trading activity and ancillary services.

### Option

A contract wherein one party (the option writer) grants another party (buyer) the right to demand that the writer perform a certain act.

*See* Call Option; Listed (Stock) Option; Put Option.

### Optional Redemption

An optional call provision reserved by the issuer that becomes exercisable after a certain number of years from issue date. This provision allows the "clean-up" of small amounts of remaining principal with thin marketability.

### Option Class

All call options or all put options (not both) having the same underlying security.

### Option Clearing Corporation (OCC)

A corporation owned jointly by all the exchanges trading listed options. On the basis of compared trades submitted by various exchanges, the OCC issues the option to the buyer and holds the writer to his or her obligation. The OCC is therefore the issuer of all listed options, and a holder must exercise against the OCC, not the original writer. The OCC maintains a system for collecting and remitting funds in settlement of option trades, and it holds collateral deposited by option writers to guarantee their performance.

### Option Premium

The fee paid by a purchaser of an option to entice someone to give him or her the right of exercise any time within a specified period. Premium is composed of intrinsic value and time premium.

*See* Net Premium.

### Option Pricing Curve

A graph of the projected prices of an option at given points in time, reflecting the amounts of time value premium in the option for various stock prices.

*See* Delta; Hedge Ratio; Model.

### Options Principal Member (OPM)

A person who buys or sells listed options on the exchange floor.

### Option Series

All options (either as a put or a call) having the same type of underlying security, strike price, and expiration date.

### Option Spreading

A system of strategies calling for the simultaneous purchase and sale of options of the same class in order to establish hedged positions.

### Option Type

The type of option as defined in the Options Clearing Corporation prospectus; calls are one type of option and puts are another.

### Option Writer

The seller of a securities option who receives an immediate fee for providing a purchaser with the right to demand performance in a securities transaction. The writer incurs an obligation to sell stock (call writer) or to purchase stock (put writer).

### Order Book Official (OBO)

An order book official is an employee of an options exchange and performs all the duties of a board broker. He is compensated by a salary paid by the exchange.

### Order Department

A group that routes buy and sell instructions to the trading floors of the appropriate stock exchanges and executes orders in the OTC market for trading accounts of both firms and customers.

### Order Room

The area occupied by the order department.

### Organization for Economic Cooperation and Development (OECD)

A group of 24 industrialized countries, based in Paris and organized to promote world trade and economic stability.

### Originator

One who originates or issues mortgage-backed securities. Builders, brokers, and others are solicited to obtain applications for mortgage loans. The individual mortgage banker who performs this function is also designated as the originator or the issuer.

### OSJ

*See* Office of Supervisory Jurisdiction.

### OTC Margin Stock

A stock traded over-the-counter whose issuer meets certain criteria that qualify the stock for margined purchases or short sales, as governed by Regulation T.

### Out for a Bid

In the municipal bond market, the securities are "out for a bid" when a dealer lends them to an agent who then attempts to sell them.

### Out of the Money

A term used to describe an option that has no intrinsic value. An option is out of the money if the striking price is unprofitable in comparison with the current market value of the underlying stock.

### Outright Purchases or Sales

The net purchases or sales made by the Federal Open Market Committee, including buys and sells that may be partially offset by repo or reverse repo agreements.

### Overcollateralization

The extent to which the bond value of the assets or the cash flow produced by the assets (collateral) exceeds the liability or the cash flow required to meet liability obligations. It is usually expressed as a percentage of par amount of the liability.

### Overlapping Debt

A bond having two issuers.

*See* Double-Barrelled Bond.

### Overnight Position

The inventory in a security at the end of the trading day.

### Oversold

In technical analysis, a security that is expected to go down in price or that went down too fast. This situation usually manifests itself as a "gap" or a "selling climax," where the closing price of a security is much below the previous day's close.

### Over-the-Counter Option (OTC)

A market, conducted mainly over the telephone, for securities made up of dealers who may or may not be members of a securities exchange. Thousands of companies have insufficient shares outstanding, stockholders, or earnings to warrant listing on a national exchange. Securities of these companies are therefore traded in the over-the-counter market between dealers who act neither as agents for their customers or as principals. The over-the-counter market is the principal market for U.S. government and municipal bonds and for stocks of banks and insurance companies.

A market for options traded directly between buyer and seller, unlike a listed stock option. These options have no secondary market and no standardization of striking prices and expiration dates.

*See* Listed Stock Option; Secondary Market.

### Overtrading

A practice in violation of NASD principles. A broker/dealer overpays a customer for a security to enable the customer to subscribe to another security offered by that broker/dealer at a higher markup than the loss to be sustained when the firm sells the customer's first security at prevailing market prices.

### Overvalued

In securities trading, a security whose market price is higher than it should be in the opinion of fundamental analysts.

In options trading, a security trading at a higher price than that indicated by the mathematical models.

*See* Fair Value; Undervalued.

### OW

*See* Offer Wanted.

### Overwriting

The act of a call writer who writes a call based on the notion that the underlying security is overpriced and will have to drop in price. If it doesn't, the call writer will suffer a loss.

### P/E Ratio

*See* Price/Earnings (P/E Ratio).

### Paid-In-Capital (Capital Surplus)

The difference between par, or bookkeeping, value of a security and the amount realized from the sale or distribution of those shares by the corporation.

### Painting the Tape

An individual or group making numerous transactions without any real change in ownership. The purpose is to dupe investors into thinking the security is being actively traded and joining in that activity.

### Paired Shares

When the common stock of two companies that are run by the same management is sold as one unit, it is said to be "paired," "stapled," or "Siamese."

### Pair Off

The matching of buys and sells to facilitate settlement for similar TBAs that settle in the same month and also for similar pools.

### P&I

*See* Principal and Interest.

## P&S Department

*See* Purchase and Sales (P&S) Department.

## Paper

Relatively short-term debt securities.

## Paper Loss/Profit

An unrealized loss or profit on a security still held. Paper losses and profits become actual when a security position is closed out by a purchase or sale.

## Par Cap

In GNMA futures contracts, a seller may not deliver substitute certificates with an interest coupon rate that requires adjusting the contract's dollar price above the issue's par value.

## Par Option

A provision in an option allowing the issuer to call securities at par.

## Parity

If no priority exists, the right of an execution is awarded to the broker who can at least completely fill the contra order. If more than one broker can fill the order, they match coins to determine who will satisfy the order.

*See* Precedence; Preference; Priority.

Options are considered to be at parity when the striking price plus the premium (less the premium for a put option) equals the market price of the underlying stock.

## Parity Bonds

Any two or more issues having the same priority of claim or lien against pledged revenues.

## Parking

The practice by a dealer of selling a security to another dealer to reduce the seller's net capital. The securities are sold back to the first dealer when a buyer is found, and the second dealer recoups any carrying charges.

## Partial Delivery

A delivery of fewer securities than the amount contracted for in the sales transaction.

### Participate But Do Not Initiate (PNI) Order

On large orders to buy or sell, an instruction given to a broker from institutional buyers or sellers not to initiate a new price, but either to let the market create a new price or obtain a favorable price through gradual and intermittent transactions. This allows the buyers or sellers to accumulate or distribute shares without disturbing the market forces. This could also be done by institutions that are not permitted by law to create an uptick or a downtick in the market.

### Participating Mortgage

A loan agreement providing that the lender receive a share of the revenue or profits, or a portion of some other defined amount, regularly received by the borrower in addition to normal debt service.

### Participating Preferred Stock

A preferred stock that is entitled not only to its stated dividend, but also to additional dividends on a specified basis if dividends are declared after payment of dividends on common stock. Usually, extra dividends are shared equally by common and participating preferred stockholders.

### Participating Trust

A unit investment company that issues shares reflecting an interest in a specified investment company.

### Participation Certificate (PC)

A form of mortgage-backed security payment that represents an undivided certain interest in estate loans.

An instrument that evidences an undivided interest in home and multifamily mortgages, and obligations secured thereby.

### Participation Interest

As evidenced by a participation certificate, a percentage of undivided interest in each mortgage and the related mortgage note.

### Partnership

A type of business organization typified by two or more proprietors.

### Par (Value)

The face or nominal value of a security.

A dollar amount assigned to a share of common stock by the corporation's charter. At one time, it reflected the value of the original investment behind each share, but today it has little significance except for bookkeeping purposes.

Many corporations do not assign a par value to new issues. For preferred shares or bonds, par value has importance insofar as it signifies the dollar value on which the dividend/interest is figured and the amount to be repaid upon redemption.

Preferred dividends are usually expressed as a percentage of the stock's par value.

The interest on bonds is expressed as a percentage of the bond's par value.

*See* Face Value.

### Pass-Back

A feature of a collateralized bond that provides that some fraction (possibly all) of the "excess" cash flow from collateral is passed to the issuer.

### Pass-Forward

A feature of a collateralized bond that provides some portion (possibly all) of the "excess" cash flow from collateral is used to redeem outstanding bond principal. Excess cash flow consists of proceeds from collateral beyond that required to maintain the overcollateralization ratio.

A form of mortgage-backed security payment whereby principal and interest are passed to the investor on a monthly basis.

### Pass-Through (P/T) Security (Bond)

A debt security representing an interest in a pool of mortgages requiring monthly payments composed of interest on unpaid principal and a partial repayment of principal. Thus the payments are passed through the intermediaries, from the debtors to investors.

### Patient Money

A generic term referring to the ability of the money partner in a joint venture to defer receipt of principal payments, interest payments, or both until the operation is profitable.

### Payable Date/Pay Date

Date on which principal and interest are due to be paid to the registered owner of a security.

### Pegging

Also known as stabilization. Keeping a security's offer price at a certain level by means of a bid at or slightly below the price. Pegging is legal only in underwriting.

### Penalty Syndicate Bid

A series of restrictive financial measures written into agreements among underwriters with the purpose of discouraging resale of securities requiring stabilization. A monetary penalty helps insure distribution to investment portfolios and not to traders and speculators seeking short-term profits at the expense of the underwriters.

### Pennant

In technical analysis, a roughly triangular chart pattern whose apex points to the right. Pennants do not indicate any clear trends because the stock may rise or fall near the apex.

### Penny Stocks

Colloquial term for—but not limited to—low-priced, high-risk stocks that usually sell for less than $1 per share. These shares usually require a special margin maintenance requirement, and purchases are often limited to unsolicited orders.

### Periodic Purchase Deferred Contract

A variable annuity contract plan under which periodic payments may be applied to accumulate separate account units. Variable annuity payments are deferred until after the accumulation period.

### Perpetual Bond

A bond with no maturity date. Also called an annuity bond.

### Perpetual Warrant

A warrant with no expiration date.

### Phantom Stock Plan

An executive compensation plan that pegs bonuses to the appreciation in the market value of the firm's stock—*as if* the executives owned the stock.

### Philadelphia Plan

The issuance of equipment trust bonds in which the title to the leased equipment remains with the trustee until all of the outstanding serial maturities for the issue are retired. It would then pass to the leasing issuer of the securities.

*See* New York Plan.

### Pickup

The increased value (usually small) achieved by means of a swap of bonds with similar coupon rates and maturities at a basis price.

### Picture

The prices at which a broker/dealer or specialist is ready to trade. For example, "The picture on XYZ is 18½ to 19, 1,000 either way."

### Piggyback Registration

The inclusion of privately purchased shares in the total shares of an offering when the issuer is making a primary distribution of securities, thus combining primary and secondary distributions.

### Pink Sheets

A list of securities being traded by over-the-counter market makers, published every business day by the National Quotations Bureau. Equity securities are published separately on long pink sheets. Debt securities are published separately on long yellow sheets.

### Pipeline (Conduit) Theory

A theory of investment stating that the tax liabilities of mutual funds are avoided by passing income and profits on to a fund's stockholders as dividends and capital distributions; the tax liabilities, ultimately, are widely dispersed among and incurred by many shareholders.

### Place

A securities distribution to a buyer, either publicly or privately.

### Plan Companies

Companies that are registered with the SEC as unit investment companies and that manage offerings of extended purchase contracts involving mutual fund shares in behalf of underwriters.

### Planned Unit Development (PUD) FHLMC

A parcel of land, with property and improvements, that is owned and maintained by a homeowners association, corporation, or trust for the benefit and use of individual PUD units. The common property enhances the enjoyment of the premises and value of the property securing the PUD unit mortgage.

### PLATO

A computer-assisted instruction and testing system developed by the Control Data Corporation.

### Pledged Revenues

Monies needed for—that is, pledged to—the payment of debt service and other deposits required by a bond contract. A *net pledge* or *net revenue pledge* is a pledge that all funds remaining after certain operational and maintenance costs are paid will be used for payment of debt services. A *gross pledge* or *gross revenue pledge* states that all revenues received will be used for the debt service prior to any deductions for costs or expenses.

### "Plus" (+)

When added to the dollar price quote for government securities, it signifies an additional 1/64.

### Plus Tick

A transaction on a stock exchange at a price higher than the price of the last transaction. Also known as an uptick.

### Plus-Tick Rule

An SEC rule stating that a short sale of a round lot has to be made at a price that was an advance over the last different regular-way sale of that security. For example, if the last transaction was at 40, the next short sale must be at 40⅛ or higher. If the last sale was itself an advance, then a sale at the same price is a zero-plus tick and legitimate for a short sale. For example, if the last two transactions were at 40 and 40⅛, then the next sale could be at 40⅛—a zero-plus tick.

### PNI Order

*See* Participate But Do Not Initiate (PNI) Order.

### Point

In stocks, $1.

In bonds, since a bond is quoted as a percentage of $1,000, it means $10. For example, a municipal security discounted at 3½ points equals $35. It is quoted at 96½ or $965 per $1,000.

In market averages, it means simply a point—a unit of measure.

### Point and Figure (P&F) Chart

In technical analysis, a chart of price changes in a security. Upward price changes are plotted as "X's," and downward prices are plotted as "O's." Time is *not* reflected on this type of chart.

### Poison Pill

Any kind of action taken by a takeover target company to make its stock less palatable to an acquirer. Tactics include issuing new preferred stocks that give shareholders the right to redeem at a premium price if a takeover does occur. This makes acquisition much more expensive for the would-be acquirer.

### Pool

Individual mortgages packaged into groups by primary lenders, such as banks, savings and loan associations, and mortgage companies.

For Fannie Mae, all mortgages purchased pursuant to one or more pool purchase transactions which will secure an individual issue of guaranteed mortgage pass-through certificates.

### Pool Number

The specific number referencing the name of a security, its terms and the issuer.

### Pool Purchase Contract (FNMA)

A contract between FNMA and a lender to buy and sell mortgages for inclusion in a pool. The pool purchase contract is uniquely identified by a number assigned by FNMA and appearing on the face of the contract.

### Pool Purchase Transaction (FNMA)

Any transaction between FNMA and a lender in which FNMA has purchased a group of mortgages from the lender for the sole purpose of backing, in whole or in part, an issue of guaranteed mortgage pass-through certificates.

### Pool Transaction Amount

The aggregate issue date principal balance of all mortgages purchased in a pool purchase transaction.

### Portfolio

Holdings of securities by an individual or institution. A portfolio may include preferred and common stocks, as well as bonds, of various enterprises.

### Portfolio Theory

A theory based on an investment approach that permits investors to classify, estimate, and control the kind and amounts of return and risk in their own portfolios.

### POS

*See* Preliminary Official Statement.

### Position

The status of securities in an account—long or short.

To buy or sell a block of securities so that a position is established.

*See* Facilitation Strategy.

### Position Limit

The maximum amount of put or call contracts placed on the same side of the market being held by any one account or group of related accounts. Short puts and long calls are placed on the same side of the market; short calls and long puts are also placed together.

### Post 30

On the floor of the NYSE, a numbered post where low-activity preferred shares are traded in round lots of 10 shares.

### Pot, The

A pool of securities, aside from those distributed among individual syndicate members, that is allocated by the manager for group or institutional sales. When "the pot is clean," the portion of the issue reserved for institutional (group) sales has been completely sold.

### Pot is Clean

*See* Pot, The.

### Power of Attorney

The legal right conferred by a person or institution upon another to act in the former's stead.

In the securities industry, a *limited power of attorney* given by a customer to a representative of a broker/dealer would normally give a registered representative trading discretion over the customer's account. The power is limited in that neither securities nor funds may be withdrawn from the account.

In the securities industry, an *unlimited power of attorney* given by a customer to a representative of a broker/dealer would normally give a registered representative full discretion over the conduct of the customer's account.

### Precedence

If an execution of an order cannot be awarded to a broker on the basis of priority or parity, then precedence (the order filling the largest part of the contra order) assumes that right before any others.

*See* Parity; Preference; Priority.

### Preemptive Right

*See* Subscription Privilege.

### Preference

If a broker with parity can prove he or she was in the trading crowd before competitors prior to the appearance of the contra order that initiated the trading activity, that broker assumes the privilege of executing an order first without matching coins.

### Preference Income

Taxable income that may be subject to additional federal income tax known as the minimum tax computation.

### Preference Stock

*See* Prior Preferred (Preference) Stock.

### Preferred Dividend Coverage

Net income divided by total preferred dividends.

### Preferred Stock

Owners of this kind of stock are entitled to a fixed dividend to be paid regularly before dividends can be paid on common stock. They also exercise claims to assets, in the event of liquidation, senior to holders of common stock but junior to bondholders. Holders of preferred stock normally do not have a voice in management.

### Preferred Stock Ratio

The relationship of preferred stock outstanding to the total capitalization of a corporation.

### Preliminary Agreement

An agreement between an issuing corporation and an underwriter drawn up prior to the effective date and pending a decision by the underwriter on the success potential of the new securities.

*See* Indication of Interest.

### Preliminary Official Statement (POS)

Also known as the preliminary prospectus, the preliminary version or draft of an official statement, as issued by the underwriters or issuers and subject to change prior to the confirmation of offering prices or interest rates. It is the only form of communication allowed between a broker and prospective buyer before the effective date, usually to gauge the interest of underwriters. Offers of sale or acceptance are not accepted on the basis of a preliminary statement. A statement to that effect, printed in red, appears vertically on the face of the document. This caveat, required by the Securities Act of 1933, is what gives the document its nickname, "red herring."

### Preliminary Prospectus

*See* Preliminary Official Statement (POS).

### Premium

The amount by which the price paid for a preferred security exceeds its face value.

The total price of an option, equal to the intrinsic value plus the time value premium. To determine the total dollar premium for a single index option, the quoted premium must be multiplied by the applicable index multiplier.

The market price of a bond selling at a price above its face amount. For example, trading at "101" means that, for $1,010, one could purchase a bond that would pay $1,000 principal at maturity.

*See* Discount Bond.

### Prepaid Charge Plan

*See* Front-End (Prepaid Charge) Plan.

### Prepaid Expense

A payment or deposit made for services, facilities, or materials in advance of receipt or use. Prepaid expense is treated as an asset.

### Presold Issue

A completely sold-out issue of municipal or government securities prior to the announcement of its price or coupon rate. This practice is illegal with regard to registered corporate offerings, but it is not illegal in the primary distribution of municipals or Treasuries.

### Price Cap

In TBA transactions, a provision made by a trader that limits the price of the trade, such as $95 per $1,000 bond.

### Price/Earnings (P/E) Ratio

A ratio used by some investors to gauge the relative value of a security in light of current market conditions.

Ratio = Market Price divided by Earnings Per Share.

### Price/Equity Ratio

The ratio of the market price of a common share to the book value of a common share.

### Price Range

The range defined by the high and low prices of a security over a given period.

### Price Spread

*See* Vertical Spread.

### Primary Distribution (Offering)

The original sale of a company's securities. The sale of authorized but unissued shares of stock is a primary sale, while the resale of Treasury shares is a secondary sale.

### Primary Earnings Per Share

A computation of earnings applicable to each share of common stock outstanding based on the supposition that all securities equivalent to common stock were exchanged for common stock at the beginning of that accounting period.

### Primary Market

Organized stock exchanges.

The new issue market as opposed to the secondary market.

### Primary Movement

A long-term (one- to five-year) movement or direction in the market.

### Primary Residence

According to FHLMC, residential property physically occupied by an owner as the principal home. Among the criteria evaluating whether a property qualifies as a principal home are: (a) It is occupied by the owner for the major portion of the year. (b) It is in a location relatively convenient to the owner's principal place of employment. (c) It is the address of record for activities such as federal income tax reporting, voting registration, occupational licensing and other functions.

### Prime Rate

The interest rate charged by a bank on loans made to its most creditworthy customers.

### Principal

*See* As Principal.

### Principal (Balance)

The amount of a debt investment minus the interest.

For a mortgage-backed security, the amortized value of the security multiplied by the price of the trade.

### Principal Distribution Amount

For a mortgage pool, the total of (a) the aggregate principal portions of the monthly installments due during the period beginning on the second day of the month preceding the month in which a remittance date occurs and ending on the first day of the month in which a remittance date occurs, whether or not collected, and (b) the aggregate unscheduled principal recoveries collected on mortgages in the pool during the month preceding the month in which a remittance date occurs.

### Principal and Interest

Payments of principal and interest made to registered holders of mortgage-backed securities.

### Principal Prepayment

Any payment or other recovery of principal on a mortgage loan that is received in advance of its scheduled due date, including any prepayment penalty or premium, and not accompanied by any interest coming due on or after the month of prepayment.

### Principal Registration

A form of registration with the NASD entitling the registrant to participate in all phases of the member organization except preparation and approval of the financial statements and net capital computations.

*See* Financial Principal; Representative Registration.

### Principal Trade

Any transaction in which the dealer or dealer bank effecting the trade takes over ownership of the securities.

### Principal Transaction

*See* As Principal.

### Principals (Stockholders)

The investors in a corporation with an equity interest, entitled to voting privileges, dividends, access to books and records, ready transferability of stock, proportionate shares of assets in liquidation, and subscription privileges.

### Principal Value

The face value of an obligation that must be repaid at maturity and that is separate from interest. Often called simply "principal."

### Prior Issue

Term applied to an outstanding issue of bonds when they are to be refinanced by a refunding.

Previous bond issues that normally possess a first, or senior, lien on pledged revenues.

### Prioritization

The ordering of security classes according to the sequence in which they are to be redeemed, such as in a multiclass bond issue.

### Priority

The privilege of the first broker in the trading crowd to execute his or her order at a particular price before any competitors. If no priority exists, then parity, precedence, or preference may be used to award the execution.

*See* Parity; Preference; Precedence.

### Prior Lien Bond

A bond that takes precedence over all other bonds from the issuer because they hold a higher-priority claim. These bonds are usually issued as a result of reorganizations arising from bankruptcy proceedings.

### Prior Preferred Stock

Preferred stock whose claim on corporate assets takes precedence over other issues of preferred stock should the issuer be dissolved. It also has priority on its claim on earnings when dividends are declared.

### Prior Preferred (Preference) Stock

A kind of preferred stock entitling the owner to prior claim to forthcoming dividends or claim to assets in liquidation proceedings.

### Private Placement

The distribution of unregistered securities to a limited number of purchasers without the filing of a statement with the SEC. Such offerings generally require submission of an investment letter to the seller by all purchasers.

### Proceeds Sale

A secondary market sale whose proceeds are used for another purchase. The two transactions are considered as one transaction, and the total sales charges must be less than 5 percent.

*See* Five Percent Guideline; Switch (Contingent or Swap) Order.

### Profit and Loss Statement (P&L)

*See* Earnings Report.

### Profit Graph

A graph which represents the potential outcome of a strategy. Dollars of profit or loss are graphed on the vertical axis while various stock prices are graphed on the horizontal axis so that results may be depicted at any point in time. The graph usually depicts the results at expiration of the options involved in the strategy.

### Profit Margin Ratio

A comparison of operating income to net sales.

### Profit Range

The area in which a position makes a profit. The term usually refers to strategies that have two breakeven points—an upside and a downside breakeven. The range between the two points is the profit range.

*See* Breakeven Point.

### Profit Table

A table showing the results of a strategy at a given point in time. It is usually a tabular compilation of the same data drawn on a profit graph.

### Profit Taking

A dropoff in general market prices after a sharp increase, in the absence of any adverse socioeconomic influence. Traders are assumed to be taking short-term profits.

### Program Buying

In whole loans, creating demand in a specific product by recommending and executing an investment strategy for a client.

## Project Loan Pass-Throughs (PLs)

A mortgage backed by a real estate project development; converse to a single-family (SF) dwelling mortgage loan. PLs are backed by GNMA.

## Proportionate Share of Assets in Liquidation

The right of a holder of common stock to assets in proportion to his or her interest, upon liquidation, after all liabilities have been satisfied.

## Proprietary

A term applied to the assets of a brokerage firm and those of its principals that have been specifically pledged as their capital contribution to the organization.

## Proprietary Account

An account used by broker/dealers for trading securities, options, or commodities for their own account and risk, as opposed to trading for their customers.

## Proprietorship (Individual)

A type of business structure consisting of one owner, who is personally responsible for all debt liabilities but who also can manage the business as he or she sees fit.

## Prospectus

A document that contains material information for an impending offer of securities (containing most of the information included in the registration statement) and that is used for solicitation purposes by the issuer and underwriters.

## Protected Strategy

A position having limited risk, such as a short sale or a protected straddle write.

*See* Combination; Straddle Option.

## Provisional Rating

With regard to a bond that is related to construction of some sort, an indication during the construction period of the bond issue's quality.

## Proxy

A formal authorization (power of attorney) from a stockholder that empowers someone to vote in his or her behalf.

The person who is so authorized to vote on behalf of a stockholder.

### Proxy Contest

The situation in which a person or group of people, other than a company's management, attempts to solicit shareholders' proxies, usually to change the management of the company.

### Proxy Department

The department in a brokerage firm responsible for soliciting proxies from beneficial owners, collecting proxies from various sources, and voting those proxies in accordance with the rules of various authorities, including the SEC and the New York Stock Exchange.

### Proxy Statement

Material information required by the SEC to be given to a corporation's stockholders as a prerequisite to solicitation of votes. It is required for any issuer subject to the provisions of the Securities Exchange Act of 1934.

### Prudent Man Investing

Investing in a fashion that is exemplified by the conduct of a conservative person managing his or her own assets. In certain cases this type of investing is limited to "legal list." Some states use the "prudent man" rule as a legal guideline for investing others' money.

### Public Book (of Orders)

A book that contains the buy or sell orders entered by the public away from the current market and that is kept by the board broker or a specialist. Only the specialist knows at what price and in what quantity the nearest public orders are.

*See* Board Broker; Market Maker; Specialist.

### Publicly Held

Term applied to a corporation whose shares are traded according to either SEC rules or New York Stock Exchange rules.

### Public Offering (Distribution)

The offering of securities for sale by an issuer.

### Public Relations and Investor Services Department

The department of the NYSE responsible for, besides public relations and investor services, almost all the advertising and public communications practices of members and member organizations.

### Pull

To turn a firm bid or offer into a subject one.

### Purchase Acquisition

The acquisition of one company by another by outright purchase. The purchase can entail cash or Treasury stock bought within the two years prior to acquisition.

### Purchase and Sales (P&S) Department

The department in operations responsible for the first processing of a trade. Responsibilities include the recording of order executions, figuring monies due and payable as a result of trades, preparing customer confirmations, and making trade comparisons with other brokers.

### Purchase Contract

A contract between seller and Freddie Mac covering the purchase, in whole or in part, of a specific dollar amount of home mortgages or multifamily mortgages.

### Purchase Group

Investment bankers who, as a group, purchase a new issue for resale to the public. The purchase group (or syndicate) differs from the selling group, another group of investment bankers whose function is distribution.

*See* Syndicate; Underwriting Agreement.

### Purchasing (Buying) Power

The amount of security value available in a margin account solely from the use of existing equity in excess of current federal requirements.

### Pure Hedge

A buying hedge used to lock in an interest rate and thereby protect against a decline in interest rates.

### Purpose Loan

A loan, using corporate securities as collateral, that is used to purchase, trade, or carry margin securities.

*See* Nonpurpose Loan.

### Purpose Statement

A form completed by a borrower and filed with a lender when margin securities are used to collateralize a loan. In this statement, the broker/dealer's customer (the borrower) expresses the purpose of the loan and guarantees that the loan proceeds are not going to be used to purchase, carry, or trade securities.

### Put Option

A privilege giving its holder the right to demand acceptance of his or her delivery of 100 shares of stock at a fixed price any time within a specified lifetime. Sometimes referred to as a seller's option.

### Pyramiding

Using profit generated by a position to add to that position.

### Q-Tip Trust

*See* Qualified Terminable Interest.

### Qualified Legal Opinion

A conditional affirmation of a security's legality, which is given before or after the security is sold. An unqualified legal opinion (called a *clean opinion*) is an unconditional affirmation of the legality of securities.

### Qualified Stock Option

An option granted to an employee by a corporation, entitling the employee to purchase capital stock at a special price, usually lower than its market value.

### Qualified Terminable Interest (Q-Tip Trust)

The transfer of assets between spouses. The creator leaves income from assets to the spouse. Upon the spouse's death, the assets are left to one or more third parties.

### Questioned Trade

*See* DK.

### Quick Asset Ratio

*See* Acid Test Ratio.

## Quick Assets

The sum of a corporation's cash, cash equivalents, and accounts receivable.

## Quotation or Quote

*See* Bid-and-Asked Quotation (or Quote).

### Radar Alert

Watching trading patterns in a particular stock to uncover any unusual buying activity, which may be signaling a takeover attempt.

*See* Shark Watcher.

### Raiders

Persons or groups of persons who attempt to buy a controlling share in a company's stock for the purpose of voting in new management, not for investment purposes.

*See* Bear Raider.

### Rally

A brisk rise following a decline in the general price level of the market or in the price of an individual stock.

### RAN

*See* Revenue Anticipation Note.

### R&D

*See* Receive and Deliver (R&D) Section.

### Random Walk Theory

A hypothesis stating that historical prices, because they react to random influences on the market, are of no use in forecasting price movements. Espoused in 1900 by the French mathematician, Louis Bachelier and revived in the sixties, this theory contradicts the principles used in technical analysis.

*See* Technical Analysis.

### Range

A set of prices consisting of the opening sale, high sale, low sale, and latest sale of the day for a given security.

### Rate of Return

In fixed income investment, *see* Current Yield.

In corporate financing, *see* Return on Equity.

### Rating Agencies

Organizations that publicly rate the credit quality of securities issuers, the most often cited being Moody's Investor's Service, Inc. and Standard & Poor's Corporation.

### Ratio Calendar Combination

A strategy that uses a simultaneous position of a ratio calendar spread using calls combined with a similar position using puts. The striking price of the calls is greater than the striking price of the puts.

### Ratio Calendar Spread

In this spread, you sell near-term options and buy longer-term options (either puts or calls), but the short-term outnumber the long-term.

### Ratio Spread

A ratio consisting of buying a certain amount of options and selling a larger number of out-of-the-money options. This strategy can be used with both puts and calls.

### Ratio Strategy

A strategy involving unequal numbers of long and short securities, generally with a preponderance of short options over either long options or long stock.

### Ratio Write

The process of buying stock and then selling a preponderance of calls against that stock. This is often constructed by shorting stock and selling puts.

### RE-1 Form

A form used by a member firm to request registration by the NYSE for an employee. It includes comprehensive disclosure of the applicant's business background and personal history.

### RE-4 Form

A form used by a member firm to request the NYSE to terminate registration of one of its employees who has left the organization.

### Reading the Tape

Appraising a security's performance by monitoring the price changes on the ticker.

### Ready Transferability of Shares

A shareholder's right to give away or sell shares without prior consultation with corporate directors.

### Real Estate Investment Trust (REIT)

A closed-end investment company investing in various ventures related to real estate.

### Real Estate Separate Acts

An investment vehicle, similar to a mutual fund, in which various types of real estate provide the security and the income. Account are usually open-ended, that is, property and participants may be added.

### Receive and Deliver (R&D) Section

Department of a brokerage house that accepts certificates directly from customers, brokers, or various securities depositories in the U.S. They also make sure all accounts are properly credited after the securities have been determined to be in transferable form.

### Receiver-in-Bankruptcy

An impartial, court-appointed administrator of a corporation that has sought protection from its creditor's claims under federal bankruptcy laws. This administrator is appointed to help the court decide between liquidation or reorganization and is remunerated out of the remaining assets of the corporation.

### Receiver's Certificates

Short-term (90- to 120-day) debt obligations issued by a receiver for a bankrupt corporation to supply working capital during the receiver's inquiry. These obligations take priority over the claims of all other creditors.

### Receive Versus Payment (RVP)

The long sale of securities in a cash account with the instructions to pay the seller upon the delivery of the securities to the broker/dealer.

*See* COD Trade.

### Reciprocal Immunity Doctrine

A court decision that neither the federal government nor states can tax income received from securities issued by the other. A state cannot tax income from Treasury securities or federal agency obligations, and the federal government cannot tax income from state-issued securities.

### Reclamation

The privilege of a seller in a transaction to recover his or her certificates and return the contract money, or of a buyer to recover his or her contract money and return the certificates, should any irregularity be discovered upon delivery and settlement of the contract.

*See* Rejection.

### Record Date

*See* Date of Record.

### Recourse Loan

A loan to a limited partnership, usually for the financing of a tax shelter. The lender has recourse not only to the partnership's assets, but also to the general partner's personal assets.

### Red Book

*See* Dealer Book.

### Redemption

For bonds, the retirement of the securities by repayment of face value or above (that is, at a premium price) to their holders.

For mutual funds, the shareholder's privilege of converting his or her interest in the fund into cash—normally at net asset value.

### Redemption Notice

A publicly issued notice stating an issuer's intent to redeem securities.

### Redemption Provision

*See* Catastrophe (Calamity) Call.

### Red Herring

*See* Preliminary Official Statement (POS).

### Rediscount

A situation in which a member bank of the Federal Reserve System borrows funds from the Federal Reserve using eligible collateral. This collateral, in turn, came from one of the bank's borrowers.

### Refunding (Refinancing)

The issuance of a new debt security, using the proceeds to redeem either older bonds at maturity or outstanding bonds issued under less favorable terms and conditions.

### Reg G

*See* Regulation G.

### Registered as to Interest Only

Bonds that are registered as to interest and on which interest checks are sent to the registered owner, but that are payable to the bearer at maturity.

### Registered as to Principal Only

Bonds that are registered and that are payable at maturity to the registered holder, but that have coupons attached that must be presented by the bearer periodically for payment.

### Registered Bond

An outstanding bond whose owner's name is recorded on the books of the issuing corporation. Legal title may be transferred only when the bond is endorsed by the registered owner.

### Registered Clearing Agency

An organization that, in accordance with Section 17A of the Securities Exchange Act of 1934, provides systems for confirming, comparing, clearing, and settling securities transactions.

### Registered Company

A corporation that is registered with the SEC and that has to file certain periodic reports, as well as reports of special importance.

### Registered Competitive Market Maker

An NYSE member who can trade for his or her own account, in addition to trad-

ing for the firm's account. These members are obliged to support the specialists in maintaining an orderly market.
*See* Specialist.

### Registered Competitive Trader

An NYSE member who, like the market maker, can trade for his or her own account, as well as for the firm's account, but usually for profits. They are, however, subject to more confining rules than the market makers.

### Registered Equity Market Maker

The American Stock Exchange counterpoint of the NYSE's registered competitive market maker.

### Registered Form

A term applied to securities that are issued in a form allowing the owner's name to be imprinted on the certificate and that allow the issuer to maintain records as to the identity of the owners. Opposite of bearer form.

### Registered Options Principal (ROP)

An individual who has been approved by an options exchange to supervise the conduct of customers' accounts in which there are listed options transactions.

### Registered Options Representative

A broker/dealer employee who has passed the examinations required before soliciting options trading orders.

### Registered Principal

*See* Principal Registration.

### Registered Representative

*See* Account Executive.

### Registered Secondary Distribution

An offering of securities by affiliated persons that requires an effective registration statement to be on file with the SEC before distribution may be attempted.

### Registered Security

A certificate (stock or bond) clearly inscribed with the owner's name.

A stock or bond that is registered with the SEC at the time of its sale. If such an initial registration does not take place, then the term also includes any security sold publicly and in accordance with the SEC's rules.

### Registered (Floor) Trader

A member of the NYSE who buys and sells stocks for his or her own account and risk.

### Registrar

Often a trust company or bank, the registrar is charged with the responsibility of preventing the issuance of more stock than authorized by the company. It insures that the transfer agent issues exactly the same number of shares cancelled with each reregistration of certificates.

### Registration Statement

A document required to be filed with the SEC by the issuer of securities before a public offering may be attempted. The Securities Act of 1933 mandates that it contain all material and accurate facts. Such a statement is required also when affiliated persons intend offering sizable amounts of securities. The SEC examines the statement for a 20-day period, seeking obvious omissions or misrepresentations of fact.

### Reg T Call

A notice to a customer of a broker/dealer that additional equity is needed in his or her account to meet the minimum standards set by Regulation T of the Federal Reserve.

### Reg T Excess

The amount of equity in a customer's account above the minimum requirements of Regulation T of the Federal Reserve.

### Reg U

*See* Regulation U.

### Regular Specialist

A specialist of the NYSE who continually solicits and executes orders in listed stocks assigned to him or her. The specialist also maintains an orderly market and provides price continuity by means of transactions for his or her own account and risk.

*See* Associate Specialists; Relief Specialist.

### Regular Way Contract

The most frequently used delivery contract. For stocks and corporate and municipal bonds, this type of contract calls for delivery on the fifth business day after the trade. For U.S. government bonds and options, delivery must be made on the first business day after the trade.

### Regulated Companies

Investment companies that meet certain criteria for eligibility and are therefore exempted by the IRS from paying taxes on investment income after expenses.

### Regulated Commodities

Commodities that are regulated by the Commodities Futures Trading Commission (CFTC), that is, all commodities traded in organized contract markets.

*See* Commodities Futures Trading Commission.

### Regulation A

A "short" filing with the SEC permitting insiders to sell a limited amount of stock.

### Regulation G

A Federal Reserve Board regulation requiring any person, other than a bank or broker/dealer, who extends credit secured directly or indirectly with margin securities, to register and be subject to Federal Reserve Board jurisdiction.

### Regulation Q

The Federal Reserve Board's interest rate on time deposits.

### Regulation T

A Federal Reserve Board regulation that explains the conduct and operation of general and special accounts within the offices of a broker/dealer firm, prescribing a code of conduct for the effective use and supervision of credit.

### Regulation U

A Federal Reserve Board regulation that regulates the extension of credit by banks when securities are used as collateral.

*See* Nonpurpose Loan; Purpose Loan.

### Regulation W

The regulation of the Federal Reserve Board pertaining to installment loans.

### Regulation X

A set of rules established by the Federal Reserve Board that places equal burdens of responsibility for compliance with Regulations G, T, and U on the borrower as well as the lender.

### Rehypothecation

A broker's practice of pledging customer securities from a margin account to serve as collateral at a bank in order to finance the customer's debit balance in this account.

### REIT

*See* Real Estate Investment Trust.

### Rejection

The privilege of the purchaser in a transaction to refuse a delivery lacking in negotiability or presented in the wrong denominations, without prejudice to his or her rights in the transaction.

*See* Reclamation.

### Relief Specialist

A specialist of the NYSE affiliated with regular specialists and capable of substituting for that specialist for a limited period. The relief specialist has the same responsibility as the regular specialist while substituting for him or her.

### Remittance Date

The 25th day of the month, or whatever day is deemed as such, or if that day is not a business day, the first business day immediately following.

### Reoffering Sale

Listed by date of maturity, the prices and yields of securities offered by the underwriters.

### Reopening an Issue

The offering by the Treasury of additiona l securities in an issue that's been already offered and sold. The new securities have the same terms and conditions, but they sell at the prevailing prices.

### Reorganization Department

The department in a brokerage firm responsible for effecting the conversion of securities, as well as completing the execution of rights and warrants, tender offers, and other types of conversions. For example, when a customer who owns convertible bonds wishes to convert them and use them to fulfill a sale of the underlying common stocks, the reorganization department would accomplish the conversion.

### Repeat Prices Omitted

A ticker tape announcement to signify that the tape has fallen three minutes behind transactions on the trading floor. Sequential transactions at the same price are then purposely eliminated from the tape; only the first trade prices in a string of transactions appear.

### Repo

*See* Repurchase Agreement.

### Representations to Management

When any member of the NYSE or person associated with a member wishes to represent a corporation or its stockholders, that person must meet certain rules established by the exchange.

### Representative Registration

The minimum NASD qualification for solicitors of investment banking or securities business, traders, assistant officers of member firms, and training directors and assistants.

*See* Financial Principal; Principal Registration.

### Repricing

Closing out a term or open repo/reverse, and reopening another with the same collateral. Thus the lender and borrower clear up any substantial changes in market value (against the original haircut) and both the accrued coupon and accrued financing interest.

### Repurchase Agreement (Repo)

A Federal Open Market Committee arrangement with a dealer in which it contracts to purchase a government or agency security at a fixed price, with provision for its resale at the same price at a rate of interest determined competitively. Used by dealers in government and municipal securities to reduce carrying costs. This transaction is not legal for nonexempt securities.

A method of financing inventory positions by sale to a nonbank institution with the agreement to buy the position back.

### Required Net Yield

The amount of interest to be received by Freddie Mac from each mortgage loan purchased as set forth in the purchase contract.

### Reserve City Bank

A commercial bank with its main office in a city where a central bank or branch is located that has net demand deposits exceeding $400 million.

### Reserve for Depletion

*See* Allowance for Depletion.

### Reserve for Depreciation

*See* Allowance for Depreciation.

### Reserve Requirement

The obligation of a commercial bank to set aside and refrain from lending a percentage of its available currency. This is a form of protection for depositors.

### Resiliency

A term to describe a specific arbitrage's performance under varying economic scenarios.

### Resistance

In technical analysis, an area above the current stock price where the stock is available in abundance and where selling is aggressive. This area is said to contain what chartists call a *resistance level.* For this reason, the stock's price may have trouble rising through the price.

*See* Support.

### Resistance Level

*See* Resistance.

### Restricted Account

A margin account in which the equity is less than the current federal requirement.

The cash account of a customer who has failed to pay for a purchase under Regulation T and must have cash in the account for a period of 90 days prior to executing a buy.

### Restricted Categories

Five categories of people outlined by the NASD Board of Governors and declared ineligible for allocations of hot issues, along with their immediate families.

### Retained Earnings

A corporation's net income after dividends have been distributed.

### Retained Earnings Statement

Appearing either as a separate schedule or as part of a balance sheet or P&L, a statement reconciling the amounts of retained earnings at the beginning and end of a period.

### Retention

The portion of an underwriter's takedown for sale to its customers. The syndicate manager holds back the balance of the takedown for institutional sales and for allocation to selling group firms that are not syndicate members.

### Retention Requirement

The amount of money necessary to be withheld in a loan after sale or withdrawal of a portion of the collateral, presently 70 percent of the proceeds of the sale, or current market value of the securities to be withdrawn.

### Retirement of Debt Securities

The repayment of principal and accrued interest due to the holders of a bond issue.

### Return

*See* Yield (Rate of Return).

### Return if Exercised

The immediate return made by a covered call writer if the underlying stock on a position is called away.

### Return if Unchanged

The return made by an investor if the underlying stock price is unchanged at the expiration of the options in the position.

### Return of Capital Dividend

A dividend paid by a corporation, in cash or kind, which is not paid from retained earnings. The striking price of a listed option is reduced by such a distribution to the nearest ⅛th dollar. The striking price of a conventional option will be reduced by the exact amount of the dividend.

### Return on Common Equity

Net profit divided by book value per share of common stock.

### Return on Equity

A corporation's net income divided by shareholder's equity.

### Return on Invested Capital

Net income plus interest expense divided by total capitalization.

### Return on Investment (ROI)

The percentage earned on a corporation's total capital. Equal to earnings before interest, taxes and dividends, divided by total capital.

### Revenue Anticipation Note (RAN)

A short-term municipal debt instrument usually offered on a discount basis. Proceeds of future revenues are pledged as collateral to the payment of the note at maturity.

### Revenue Bonds

Tax-exempted bonds whose interest payments are dependent upon, secured by, and redeemable from the income generated by a particular project financed by their issuance.

### Reversal

In technical analysis, a substantial, and/or long-term, countermovement of a trend.

### Reverse a Swap

The transaction following a bond swap that reinstates the original portfolio position—reversing the swap.

### Reversal Arbitrage

A riskless arbitrage involving the sale of the stock short, the writing of a put, and the purchase of a call with the options all having the same terms.

*See* Conversion Arbitrage.

### Reverse Conversion

A term used to describe the creation of a put option from a call option by means of taking a short position in the underlying equity.

### Reverse Hedge (Synthetic Straddle)

A strategy using the sale of the underlying stock short and the purchase of calls on more shares than are sold short. It is now considered an outmoded strategy for stocks with listed puts trading.

*See* Straddle Option; Ratio Write.

## Reverse Repurchase Agreement (Repo)

For Federal Open Market Committee transactions, synonymous with matched sale/purchase agreements.

A transaction by which a broker/dealer provides funds to customers by means of purchasing a security with a contract to resell it at the same price plus interest.

## Reverse Roll

Swap from a when-issued version of a security to the most recently issued version. Usually done about the time the when-issued is announced.

## Reverse Split

A means by which a corporation reduces the number of shares outstanding by issuing one new share for more than one old share. For example, a corporation calls all its old shares and issues one new share for each five old shares held. The purpose of such a move would be to increase the price per share in the market.

## Reverse Strategy

Any strategy that is the opposite of any better known strategy. A ratio spread, for example, is a process of purchasing calls at a low strike and then selling more calls at a higher strike. A reverse ratio spread (or backspread) is the exact opposite: selling the calls at the low strike and then purchasing more calls at the higher strike.

*See* Reverse Hedge; Ratio Write.

## Revocable Trust

An agreement that gives income-producing property to an heir and that may be altered as often as the creator pleases. The entire trust can even be cancelled or revoked.

## Rigged Market

The manipulation of a security price in an attempt to attract buyers and sellers.

*See* Manipulation.

## Right

*See* Subscription Right.

## Right of Accumulation

A privilege offered by some investment companies that allows the investor to include the total market value of shares already owned in calculating sales charges when a new investment is made in additional shares.

### Rights Offering

A right that is granted by a corporation and that enables shareholders to purchase a number of shares of a new issue of common stock, usually at a lower price than the market price of the existing shares. The offer is made to the shareholders before the issue is offered to the public.

### Ring

The circular trading area in a commodity exchange. Also called the pit.

### Rising Bottom

In technical analysis, a chart pattern, usually on a daily chart, indicating a rising trend in a security's price.

### Risk Arbitrage

A purchase and short sale of potentially equal securities at prices that may realize a profit.

*See* Bona Fide Arbitrage.

### Risk-Averse Investor

An investor who follows a theory of risk and return: the higher the amount of risk, the greater the return should be.

### Riskless Transaction

*See* Simultaneous (Riskless) Transaction.

### Roll

Swap from the most recently issued security into a when-issued version of the same security; usually done about the time that the when-issued security is announced.

### Roll Down

Closing out options at one strike while simultaneously opening other options at a lower strike.

### Roll Forward

Closing out options at a near-term expiration date and then opening options at a longer-term expiration date.

### Rolling

Any follow-up action taken by the strategist to close options currently in the position and to open other options with different terms, but on the same underlying stock.

*See* Roll Down; Roll Forward Roll Up.

### Rolling Stock

In the transportation industry, movable equipment, such as locomotives, freight cars, and the like.

### Rollover

The reinvestment of funds received from the maturity of a debt instrument into another debt instrument.

Moving funds in a tax-free transaction from one retirement plan to another.

*See* IRA Rollover.

### Roll Up

Closing out options at a lower strike and then opening options at a higher strike.

### ROP

*See* Registered Options Principal.

### Rotation

Procedure whereby bids and offers are made sequentially for each series of options on an underlying stock. This does not necessarily cover trades.

### Round Lot

A unit of trading or a multiple thereof. On the NYSE, stocks are traded in round lots of 100 shares for active stocks and 10 shares for inactive ones. Bonds are traded in units of $1,000.

*See* Normal Trading Unit; Odd Lot.

### Rounding Bottom

In technical analysis, a chart pattern suggesting the shape of a saucer. Also called a saucer. The trend is considered upward.

### Rounding Top

In technical analysis, a chart pattern suggesting the shape of an inverted saucer. A rounding top indicates a downward trend.

### RR

*See* Account Executive.

### Rule 10a-1

*See* Plus-Tick Rule.

### Rule 10b-2

No one may solicit purchases of a security while participating in a distribution of the security (SEC).

### Rule 10b-4

No one may short sell securities in response to a tender offer (SEC).

### Rule 10b-5

SEC rule making it unlawful to engage in any act, practice, or business that amounts to fraud or deceit.

### Rule 10b-6

Neither issuers, underwriters, broker/dealers, nor anyone with an interest in a securities distribution may purchase, or make others purchase, the issue before the public offering (SEC).

### Rule 10b-7

Sets the conditions enabling an underwriter to use a stabilizing bid (SEC).

### Rule 10b-8

Forbids anyone participating in a distribution from using a rights offering to manipulate a security's open market price (SEC).

### Rule 10b-10

Governs the preparation and distribution of customer confirmations.

### Rule 10b-13

Anyone making a tender offer is prohibited from purchasing the security involved until the tender offer has expired (SEC).

### Rule 10b-16

Broker/dealers, in lending money to customers, must disclose complete information about the terms (SEC).

### Rule 11A

Governs trading by exchange members for their own accounts (SEC).

### Rule 13D

Anyone coming into beneficial ownership of 5 percent or more of a registered stock must file certain disclosure statements with the SEC.

### Rule 15c2-1

Prescribes the requirements for keeping customer's securities when they are left with a broker after a purchase in a margin account.

### Rule 15c2-11

An SEC rule regulating submission and representation of quotations of little-known securities whose asset value is questionable.

### Rule 15c3-1

SEC rule governing the liquid capital that a broker/dealer must maintain in terms of aggregate indebtedness to customers. Called the "net capital" rule.

### Rule 15c3-2

Broker/dealers must advise customers, when they have credit balances in their accounts, that the credit balance may be withdrawn (SEC).

### Rule 15c3-3

*See* Bulk Identification/Segregation.

### Rule 17f-1

Stolen, lost, counterfeit, or misplaced securities must be promptly reported to the National Crime Information Center (NCIC), a central computer service (SEC).

### Rule 144

An SEC rule permitting the occasional sale of restricted ("letter") securities in modest amounts by certain persons without registration with the SEC.

### Rule 174

States when a broker/dealer must give a customer a prospectus regarding recently registered securities in a secondary market transaction (SEC).

### Rule 237

An SEC rule that permits nonaffiliated holders of restricted ("letter") securities to sell them publicly under certain conditions if they cannot dispose of them privately due to circumstances beyond their control.

### Rule 325

*See* Substantial Net Capital.

### Rule 405

An NYSE rule requiring its membership to perform a proper investigation into the financial affairs of each customer before and during a business relationship with that party. This directive is also referred to as the "know your customer" rule.

### Rule 411 (AMEX)

The American Stock Exchange's version of the "know your customer" rule of the NYSE.

### Rule 415

SEC rule concerning shelf registration permitting corporations to file a registration for securities they intend to issue in the future when market conditions are favorable.

### Rule 433

States when a broker/dealer may use a preliminary prospectus (SEC).

### Rules of Fair Practice

A set of rules established and maintained by the NASD Board of Governors regulating the ethics employed by members in the conduct of their business.

### Rule of 72

A mathematical rule for approximating the period in which an amount of money will double at a given compound interest rate. That time is equal to 72 divided by the interest rate.

### Run

A market maker's list of offerings, including bid-offer prices (and, for bonds, par values and prices).

In technical analysis, a quick movement of prices, usually in reference to an uptrend.

### Run on a Bank

A situation in which a substantial number of depositors, fearing for the safety of their funds, seek withdrawal of their balances in currency.

### Running Ahead

An AE's entering a personal buy/sell order before entering a customer's order. This activity is not ethical.

### Running Through the Pot

In a distribution, the syndicate manager can take securities back from the group members and put them into "the pot" for institutional sales. Usually this is done if institutional sales are doing better than retail sales.

*See* Pot, The.

### RVP Trade

*See* Receive Versus Payment (Trade).

**s**

A symbol on the ticker tape meaning 100 shares if preceded by a single digit—or the actual quantity if preceded by more than one digit.

For example:

T
2s50½

means 200 shares of AT&T at 50½

**s.**
**s.**

A symbol on the ticker tape meaning actual quantity in a security that trades in round lots of 10 shares.

**s.**
**t.**

A symbol on the ticker tape meaning "stopped."

**Safekeeping**

A protected condition maintained as a service by a brokerage firm for its customers' fully paid securities registered in the customers' own names. The practice entails use of vault space to store those certificates until they are withdrawn or sold.

### Sales Charge

*See* Load.

### Same Day Substitution

A provision of Regulation T of the Federal Reserve that allows a customer to sell securities and buy securities of a lesser or equal amount without having to deposit separate initial margin requirements on the purchase.

### Saturday Night Special

A sudden attempt, usually over a weekend, to take over a company by a public tender offer. The Williams Act of 1968 now restricts the use of tender offers and requires disclosure of a 5-percent-or-more ownership of any equity security.

### Saucer

*See* Rounding Bottom.

### Savings Bank

A state-chartered institution that accepts both time and demand deposits. Usually organized as a stock or mutual company, it uses its deposits to invest in mortgages, real estate, government bonds, and so on.

### Savings Bond

Bond issued through the U.S. government at a discount and in face values from $50 to $10,000. The interest is exempt from state and local taxes, and no federal tax comes due until the bond is redeemed.

*See* Series EE (Savings) Bond; Series HH (Current Income) Bond.

### Savings Deposit

An interest-earning deposit in a commercial bank subject to immediate withdrawal.

### Scale

When serial bonds are initially offered, the scale designates the various maturity dates, coupon rates, and offering prices.

### Scale Orders

Multiple limit orders entered by investors at various prices but at the same time.

The purpose is to obtain an overall, or average, favorable purchase or sale price. Multiples of round lots may be either *bought* at prices scaled down from a given value or *sold* at prices scaled up from a given value.

### Scalper

A market maker who puts heavy markups or markdowns on transactions.

*See* Five Percent Guideline.

*See* Local.

### SCC

*See* Stock Clearing Corporation.

### Schedule C

A set of criteria contained in the NASD by-laws whereby various persons associated with a member organization must qualify and register with the association as principal, financial principal, or representative.

### Schedule 13D

A schedule that persons must file within 10 business days of acquiring 5 percent or more of an SEC-registered equity security. The filers must disclose how they acquired the shares and what their purpose is.

### Schedule 13G

A shortened version of Schedule 13D, to be filed by the same persons who must file the longer version but who obviously have no intention of influencing the company.

### S Corporation

*See* Subchapter S Corporation.

### Screen (Stocks)

To look for stocks that meet certain predetermined investment and financial requirements.

### Scrip

Document evidencing the fractional share of a stock distributed by a company because of an exchange of stock, split, or spin-off. The owner can then buy the remaining fraction to make a full share.

### Seasoned Issue

An issue, once distributed, that trades actively and that has great liquidity.

### Seasoning

The aging of a mortgage. The amount of time that has elapsed since origination.

### Seat (Franchise)

A membership in an exchange. A seat must be owned by an individual who is a U.S. citizen and at least twenty-one years of age; it may be sold at auction to the highest bidder or transferred for a nominal consideration, subject to approval by the exchange's board of directors.

*See* Allied Member.

### SEC

*See* Securities and Exchange Commission.

### SECO Member

A broker/dealer who is not a member of a registered stock exchange or of the NASD. The initials stand for Securities and Exchange Commission Organization to denote the member's registration with the commission.

### Secondary Distribution (Offering)

A public offering of stock by selling it to stockholders. If listed on the NYSE, a member firm may be employed to facilitate such an offering in an over-the-counter net transaction for a purchase, with prior approval of the exchange. Both member and nonmember broker/dealers can participate in this distribution.

### Secondary Market

A term referring to the trading of securities not listed on an organized exchange.

A term used to describe the trading of securities other than a new issue.

### Secondary Movement

A short-term movement in the market in the opposite direction from the primary movement.

### Secondhand Option

*See* Special Option.

### Second Mortgage

A lien against a property that has lower priority than the primary or first mortgage.

### SEC Rules

*See* Rule + specific number.

### SEC Statement of Policy

A policy set forth by the SEC, governing fair and proper sales representations of mutual funds to the public. It encompasses both verbal and written practices employed to solicit or distribute those shares.

### Secured Obligation (Bond/Debt)

A debt whose payment of interest and/or principal is secured by the pledge of physical assets.

### Securities Act of 1933

Federal legislation designed to protect the public in the issuance and distribution of securities by providing to prospective purchasers full and accurate information about an issue.

### Securities Analysis

The historical study of stock movements and trends by means of charting. Most brokerage firms now employ an analyst to aid them in predicting the financial condition of a company or a group of companies.

### Securities and Exchange Commission (SEC)

A government agency responsible for the supervision and regulation of the securities industry.

### Securities Exchange Act of 1934

Federal legislation designed to protect the public against unfair and inequitable practices on stock exchanges and in over-the-counter markets throughout the United States.

### Securities Industry Association (SIA)

An association devoted to instructing member employees and to lobbying for the members' interests.

### Securities Industry Automation Corporation (SIAC)

A corporation owned two-thirds by the New York Stock Exchange and one-third by the American Stock Exchange. The corporation is under contract to receive trade information from the two exchanges and from their members for the purpose of assisting in final settlement. Data is also supplied to the Consolidated Tape Association (CTA), the Consolidated Quotation System (CQS), the

National Security Clearing Corporation (NSCC), and the Intermarket Trading System (ITS). To perform this function, SIAC issues balance orders and continuous net settlement information to the members.

## Securities Investor Protection Corporation (SIPC)

Formed by the Securities Investors Protection Act of 1970, a government-sponsored, private, nonprofit corporation that guarantees repayment of money and securities to customers in amounts up to $500,000 per customer in the event of a broker/dealer bankruptcy. SIPC covers up to a maximum of $500,000, only $100,000 of which may be for cash. If you have, for example, $100,000 in cash and $100,000 in securities in your account, your are covered for $200,000 ($100,000 of which is cash). If you have $200,000 in securities and $200,000 in cash, you are covered for $300,000 ($200,000 in securities plus $100,000 in cash). If you have $500,000 in securities and $100,000 in cash, you are covered for $500,000, the maximum.

## Security

A transferable instrument evidencing ownership or creditorship, such as a note, stock or bond, evidence of debt, interest or participation in a profit-sharing agreement, investment contract, voting trust certificate, fractional undivided interest in oil, gas, or other mineral rights, or any warrant to subscribe to, or purchase, any of the foregoing or other similar instruments.

## Security Balance

With respect to each mortgage in a pool, the issue date principal balance less any principal distribution amounts included in previous monthly remittances. For each pool, the aggregate security balance as of any date is equal to the aggregate issue.

## Security Districts

Thirteen administrative districts throughout the United States established by the NASD. Each district is governed by a district committee and represented on the association's Board of Governors.

## Security Ratings

Ratings set by rating services, such as Moody's, Standard & Poor's, or Fitch, denoting evaluations of the investment and credit risk attached to securities.

## Seek a Market

Look to make or buy a sale.

### Segregate

To keep customer securities physically separate from those owned by the broker/dealers.

### Segregated Securities

Customer-owned securities fully paid-for or representing excess collateral in a margin account that are locked away and cannot be used in the conduct of the firm's business.

### Segregation

A protected condition maintained by a brokerage firm for its customer's fully paid securities and those representing excess collateral in margin accounts.

*See* Rule 15c3-3.

### Seller

The owner of the mortgage loan to be sold.

### Sell the Book

An instruction to the broker/dealer to sell as many shares as possible at the best available bid.

### Seller's Option Contract

In stocks or bonds, a settlement contract by which delivery of the certificates is due at the purchaser's office on a specific date (usually within sixty calendar days of the trade date) stated in the contract at the time of purchase; expressed as "Seller's 24," "Seller's 39," and so forth.

*See* Put Option.

### Selling Concession

A fraction of an underwriter's spread granted to a selling group member by-agreement. It is payment for services as a sales agent for the underwriters.

### Selling Dividends

The unfair and unethical practice of soliciting purchase orders for mutual fund shares solely on the basis of an impending distribution by that fund.

### Selling Group

Selected broker/dealers of the NASD who contract to act as selling agents for underwriters and who are compensated by a portion of the sales charge (selling concession) on newly issued stocks. They assume no financial liability for the unsold balance, but they do not share in profit from syndicate residuals.

### Selling Off (Sell-Off)

Selling commodities or securities to avoid losses from continued drops in price.

### Selling on the Good News

Practice of selling a stock right after good news has pushed the stock price very high. The investor thinks that the stock has reached its top price.

### Sell Long

To sell securities that one hold's, that is, that one has a "long" position in.

### Sell-Out

Upon failure of the purchasing firm to accept delivery of the security and lacking the proper rejection form, the seller can without notice dispose of that security in the marketplace at the best available price and hold the buyer responsible for any financial loss resulting from the default.

*See* Buy-In.

### Sell Plus:

A market or limit order to sell a security at a price higher than the previous differently-priced transaction for that security.

### Sell Short

To sell securities that one does not own. Typically, the seller's brokerage firm arranges to borrow stock to make delivery to the buyer, until the seller "closes" the position by purchasing stock and turning it over to the brokerage firm.

### Sell Stop Order

A memorandum that becomes a market order to sell if and when someone trades a round lot at or below the memorandum price.

### Senior Options Principal (SOP)/ Senior Registered Options Principal (SROP)

The senior partner or officer of a member firm holding the ultimate responsibility for the conduct of the firm's options business.

### Separate Account

A specialized legal entity created by an insurance company to incorporate contracts offered by the company under a variable annuity plan.

### Separate Customer

As defined by SIPC, the accounts of a given customer at a single brokerage firm. Different types of accounts held by the same person do not constitute "separate customers."

### Serial Bond

An issue that matures in relatively small amounts at stated periodic intervals.

### Serial Issue

An issue of bonds with maturity dates spread out over several years.

### Series

A term referring to all option contracts having the same striking price, expiration date, and unit of trading on the same underlying stock.

### Series E Savings Bonds

Nonmarketable federal savings bonds of various denominations (minimum of $50) offered at a price below face value and redeemed at face value five years later; they have a ballooning interest rate averaging 6 percent yearly.

### Series EE (Savings) Bonds

Nontransferable U.S. government bonds that are issued in denominations of $50 to $10,000 at a discount from their face values and that mature at their face values.

### Series H Savings Bonds

Nonmarketable federal savings bonds of various denominations (minimum of $500) offered and redeemed at face value and bearing interest every six months during a lifetime of ten years.

### Series HH (Current Income) Bonds

Nontransferable U.S. government bonds that pay interest semiannually. Since 1982, available only in exchange for Series EE bonds.

### Servicer

A lender who performs the ongoing servicing activities of a mortgage pool.

### Settlement Balance Order (SBO)

The amount of a TBA trade to be processed through the MBSCC. The SBO trade must be a GNMA security in a quantity of $1 million or multiples thereof.

### Settlement (Delivery) Date

The day on which certificates involved in a transaction are due at the purchaser's office.

*See* Regular Way Contract.

Settlement of index option exercises between brokers takes place on the business day immediately following the day of exercise.

For Fannie Mae, the date of delivery of the guaranteed mortgage pass-through certificates associated with any pool purchase transaction to the lender.

### Severally and Jointly

A phrase included in a typical municipal underwriting agreement by which each member of the syndicate agrees to be fully liable for payment to the issuer upon the failure of fellow underwriters to sell their allocations to their customers. This type of relationship is called a "united" or "Eastern" account.

### Severally But Not Jointly

A phrase included in a typical corporate underwriting agreement by which each member of the syndicate agrees to be fully liable for payment to the issuer upon the failure of fellow underwriters to sell their allocations to their customers. This type of relationship is called a "united" or "Western" account.

### Severally But Not Jointly

A phrase included in a typical corporate underwriting agreement by which each member of the syndicate agrees to be liable only for its allocation of the issue and not for allocations that fellow underwriters failed to dispose of. Such a relationship is called a "dividend  or owestern" account.

### Shadow Calendar

Forthcoming issues that are registered with the SEC but that are not offered yet, usually because of a backlog at the SEC.

### Share

A stock certificate—a unit of measurement of the equity ownership of a corporation.

### Share Broker

A discount broker who charges a commission that decreases as the number of shares traded increases.

### Shareholder

*See* Principals (Shareholders); Stockholders.

### Shareholders' (Stockholders') Equity

The financial interest of the stockholders in the net assets of a company. It is the aggregate of the accounts of holders of preferred and common stock accounts, as depicted on a balance sheet.

### Shark Repellant

Any step taken by a "target" corporation to discourage a takeover. Also called a procupine provision.

*See* Poison Pill.

### Shark Watcher

A company whose business is to detect takeover attempts by watching trading patterns in a client's stock.

### Shelf Distribution

A privilege written in a registration statement enabling an affiliated person to dispose of sizable amounts of securities from his or her portfolio (shelf) over a nine-month period following the effective date. For OTC transactions, order tickets must be marked "distribution stock"; for exchange sales, "Dist."

### Shell Company (Corporation)

A corporation without assets or any apparent business activity. The purpose of the company could be to obtain financing prior to starting operations or to "front" for a tax evasion scheme.

### Shop/Shopping the Street

"Shop" is slang for the broker/dealer's office.

"Shop" or "shopping the street" means a broker/dealer's gathering quotations from OTC market makers to form a basis for negotiating a transaction.

*See* Firm Market; Subject Market; Workout Market.

### Short-Against-the-Box

A situation in which a person is both long and short in the same security at the same time in his/her account, a practice usually employed to defer tax liability on capital gains. Although the customer sells the stock short, he/she actually owns the security, which is held in the broker's "box." The aim is to protect a capital gain in owned shares, while deferring the taxes due if the shares were actually sold and the capital gain reported. This way, the investor can wait until he or she is in a more favorable tax situation to sell the securities.

### Short Interest Theory

Short Interest positions are reported each month as of the fifteenth. The theory postulates that an increase in the short interest is bullish since those customers who are short must buy back that position, causing a demand for securities. A decline in short interest would be bearish.

### Short Leg

The short option in a spread.

### Short Market Value

The market value of security positions that a customer owes to a broker/dealer (short in the account).

### Short Position

The number of shares in a given security sold short and not covered as of a particular date.

The total amount of stock sold short by all investors and not covered as of a particular date.

A term used to denote the writer of an option.

### Short Sale

The sale of a security that is not owned at the time of the trade, necessitating its purchase some time in the future to "cover" the sale. A short sale is made with the expectation that the stock value will decline, so that the sale will be eventually covered at a price lower than the original sale, thus realizing a profit. Before the sale is covered, the broker/dealer borrows stock (for which collateral is put up) to delivery on the settlement date.

### Short Selling Power

The dollar amount of equity securities a customer may sell short without additional funds and continue to meet the initial margin requirements of Regulation T of the Federal Reserve. Short selling power is equal to the Reg T excess divided by the Reg T initial margin requirements. For example, $10,000/50% = $20,000.

### Short-Stop (Limit) Order

A memorandum that becomes a limit order to sell short when someone creates a round-lot transaction at or below the memorandum price (electing sale). The short sale may or may not be executed since the rules then require that it be sold at least one-eighth above the electing sale as well as high enough in value to satisfy the limit price.

## Short-Term Capital Transaction

The sale of securities held for six months or less, or a short sale and a purchase to cover at a profit within any time period.

## SIAC

*See* Securities Industry Automation Corporation.

## Siamese Stock

*See* Paired Stock.

## Silent Partner

A member of a partnership represented only by capital and not entitled to a voice in management.

## Simple Interest

Interest calculated only on the original principal.

*See* Compound Interest.

## Simultaneous (Riskless) Transaction

A transaction in which the broker/dealer takes a position in a security only after receipt of an order from a customer, and only for the purpose of acting as principal so as to disguise his or her remuneration from the transaction.

## Single Certificate

In mortgaged-backed securities, a certificate evidencing a 100% participation interest.

## Single-Family Pass-Throughs

A loan insured by FHA or guaranteed by VA that applies to single-family dwelling mortgages. These mortgages are backed by GNMA and make up the majority of GNMA mortgage-backed securities.

## Single Purchase Immediate Contract

A variable annuity contract plan under which a single payment is made for units of the separate account. Variable annuity payments commence immediately.

## Sinker

Slang for a bond with a sinking fund.

*See* Sinking Fund.

### Sinking Fund

An annual reserve of capital required to be set aside out of current earnings to provide monies for retirement of an outstanding bond issue and, sometimes, preferred stock. Such a feature has a favorable effect on the market value of that issue.

A separate account in the overall sinking fund for monies used to redeem securities by open-market purchase, by request for tenders or call, or in accordance with the redemption schedule in the bond contract.

### SIPC

*See* Securities Investor Protection Corporation.

### Skip Date

In governments trading, settlement two business days after the trade.

### SL

Stockbroker shorthand for "Sell."

### Slate

The trader's order entry that adjusts the inventory position.

### SLD

*See* Sold Sale.

### Slow-Pay Bonds

A class of bonds that are redeemed after redemption of bonds in other classes.

### SMA

*See* Special Miscellaneous (Memorandum) Account.

### Snowballing

*See* Gathering in the Stops.

### Soft Currency/Soft Dollars

Payment by some means other than "cold hard dollars," such as underwriting credits or commissions from transactions.

### Soft Market

The market for securities with low demand.

### Soft Spot

Term used to describe the weakness in a select stock or group of stocks during a generally strong and advancing market.

### Sold Last Sale

A ticker tape identification for a transaction that has fluctuated volatilely between sales. It appears for an issue that has moved one or more points if its previous sale was 19⅞ or below, two or more points if its previous sale was 20 or above.

### Sold-Out Market

In commodities trading, the futures contracts of a particular commodity are hard to come by due to contract liquidations and limited offerings.

### Sold Sale (SLD)

A transaction appearing on the ticker tape out of its proper sequence.

### Sold to You

Term used by over-the-counter traders to confirm the acceptance of their offer.

### SOP/SROP

*See* Senior Options Principal/Senior Registered Options Principal.

### Special

A security in demand as repo collateral, which can be financed at a lower rate than general collateral.

### Special Arbitrage Account

An account in which a customer purchases a security and at about the same time either: (1) sells it in a different market or (2) sells an equal security in the same or different market to take advantage of a difference in prices. Such an account is entitled to special margin requirements under Regulation T.

### Special Assessment Bond

A municipal general obligation bond whose debt service is paid by a special tax or assessment on users of the facility.

### Special Bid

A New York Stock Exchange procedure for facilitating bids for a large block of stock. Regulations are similar to those regarding a special offer.

### Special Bond Account

An account in which a customer may favorably finance a purchase of (1) exempted securities or (2) nonconvertible bonds traded on registered stock exchanges in the United States. The account is defined in Regulation T.

### Special Cash Account

An account in which the customer is required to make full payment on the fifth business day after the trade date, and in no case later than the seventh calendar day or arrange for COD payment on the fifth business day. The account is defined in Regulation T.

*See* Frozen Account.

### Special Convertible Security Account

An account used to finance activity in debt securities that are traded on a registered stock exchange and that (1) are convertible into a margin stock or (2) carry a warrant or right to subscribe to a margin stock. The account is defined in Regulation T.

### Special Deals

A mutual fund underwriter's improper practice of disbursing anything of material value (more than $25 in value per person annually) in addition to normal discounts or concessions associated with the sale or distribution of investment company shares.

### Specialist

A member of the NYSE with two essential functions: First, to maintain an orderly market, insofar as reasonably practicable, in the stocks in which he or she is registered as a specialist. To do this, the specialist must buy and sell for his or her own account and risk, to a reasonable degree, when there is a temporary disparity between supply and demand. To equalize trends, the specialist must buy or sell counter to the direction of the market. Second, the specialist acts as a broker's broker, executing orders when another broker cannot afford the time. At all times the specialist must put the customer's interest before his own. All specialists are registered with the NYSE as regular, substitute, associate, or temporary.

### Specialist Block Purchase/Sale

With the approval of a floor official, a specialist may buy from another member firm representing an institutional investor a large block of stock for his or her own portfolio in a private over-the-counter transaction. In a purchase, the specialist buys at a price lower than the prevailing floor price. In a purchase, the specialist sells at a somewhat higher price.

### Specialist Book

The chronological notebook of NYSE specialists used to keep a record of the buy and sell orders they receive for execution at specified prices. It also includes their own inventory or securities. The book is *not* public information.

### Specialized Companies

Investment companies that concentrate their investments in one industry, group of related industries, or a single geographic area of the world for the purpose of long-term capital growth.

### Special Miscellaneous (Memorandum) Account (SMA)

An account defined under Regulation T used to record a customer's excess margin and buying power. Excess funds arise from sales proceeds, market value appreciation, dividends, or margin call cash.

### Special Obligation Bond

A bond secured by a specific revenue source.

### Special Offering

The disposal of a large block of stock in accordance with certain terms and conditions, by inviting members of the exchange to place buy orders on the floor to be executed by crossing in the normal procedure. The seller pays a special commission.

### Special Omnibus Account

A brokerage account maintained by one broker/dealer in behalf of customer transactions of another broker/dealer. Execution and clearing services are provided by the carrying firm without ever knowing the identities of the introducing firm's customers, whose activities are processed under the introducing firm's name. The account is defined in Regulation T.

### Special (Secondhand) Option

This is an over-the-counter option with some remaining lifetime that is offered for resale by a put and call broker or dealer in a secondary market transaction.

### Special Subscription Account

An account under Regulation T of the Federal Reserve in which a customer can receive favorable financing arrangements for the purpose of subscribing to new issue securities.

### Special Tax Bond

A municipal bond whose payment of interest and/or principal is contingent upon the collection of a tax imposed against those who will benefit from the use of the funds obtained from the issuance of the bond.

### Special Units

Units of three or more fully qualified specialists who have banded together in a partnership or corporation for the purpose of maintaining an orderly market in specific stocks.

### Spectail

A combination of "speculator" and "retail." A broker/dealer who does more speculative trading for his or her account than handling of client orders.

### Speculation

The employment of funds in high-risk transactions for relatively large and immediate gains in which the safety of principal or current income is of secondary importance.

### Spin Off

A distribution of stock in a company that is owned by another corporation and that is being allocated to the holders of the latter institution.

### Split

A division of outstanding shares of a corporation into a large number of shares, by which each outstanding share entitles its owner to a fixed number of new shares. Individual shareholders' overall equity remains the same, but they own more stock, since the total value of the shares remains the same. For example, in a two-for-one split, the owner of 100 shares, each worth $100, would be given 200 shares, each worth $50.

### Split Commission

When one AE executes a transaction that was brought in by another AE, they split the commission between them.

### Split Down

A corporate reorganization whereby the holder of a security must return the certificate to the issuer and receive proportionately fewer shares in exchange.

### Split Offering

An offering combining both a primary and secondary distribution.

A municipal bond offering, part of which consists of serial bonds and part of which is made up of term bonds.

### Split Order

The periodic purchase or sale of small parts of a large block of securities to avoid market upset and price fluctuations.

### Split Rating

A term used to describe the situation in which a corporation has been given different credit ratings by different services.

### Split Up

A corporate recapitalization in which the holder of a security receives proportionately more shares from the issuer in relation to his or her current ownership in the company.

### Sponsor

*See* Underwriter.

### Spot Secondary Distribution

A secondary distribution that does not require an SEC registration statement and may be attempted on the spot, without delay.

### Spread

The difference in value between the bid and offering prices.

The simultaneous purchase and sale of the same class of options.

Underwriting compensation.

### Spread Option

In the OTC market, one put and one call option carrying the same expiration date but different strike prices. The call is written with a strike price above that current value of the underlying stock, while the put is written with a strike price below that value.

The simultaneous purchase and sale of listed options of the same class.

### Spread Order

An order to execute the simultaneous purchase and sale of options of the same class for either a net debit or a net credit without regard to the prices of the individual options. Spread orders may be limit orders, not held orders, or orders with discretion but they cannot be stop orders. The spread order may be either a debit or credit.

### Spread Position

*See* Spread Option.

### Spread Strategy

Any option position on the same underlying security encompassing long and short options of the same type.

### Stabilization

The syndicate manager is empowered by the members of his group to maintain a bid in the aftermarket at or slightly below the public offering price, thus "stabilizing" the market and giving the syndicate and selling group members a reasonable chance of successfully disposing of their allocations. This practice is a legal exception to the manipulation practices outlawed by the Securities and Exchange Act of 1934.

### Stag

A speculator who buys and sells stocks rapidly for fast profits.

### Stagflation

The combination of sluggish economic growth, high unemployment, and high inflation.

### Stagnation

A period of low volume and inactive trading on a securities market.

The economic doldrums resulting from retarded economic growth.

### Standard & Poor's (S&P) Corporation

A source of investment services, most famous for its *Standard & Poor's Rating* of bonds and its composite index of 425 industrial, 20 transportation, and 55 public utility common stocks, called *Standard & Poor's Index*.

### Standby

A commitment to lend funds for a short period after completion of construction until permanent financing can be arranged.

### Standby Contract

A commitment to buy or sell a specified number of mortgage-backed securities by or on a specified date.

### Standby Commitment

*See* Standby Underwriting Agreement.

### Standby Margin

In commodity calls, the account of money deposited to ensure performance of an obligation at a future date.

### Standby Underwriting Agreement

An agreement between an investment banker and a corporation whereby the banker agrees for a negotiated fee to purchase any or all shares offered as a subscription privilege (rights offering) that are not bought by the rights holders by the time the offer expires.

### Stapled Stock

*See* Paired Stock.

### Stated Percentage Order

An order by institutional or other substantial investors to buy or sell a certain percentage of the market volume of a given security. The purpose is to avoid upsetting prices that reflect normal conditions of supply and demand.

### Statement of Purpose

A document stating the purpose of the loan required of a borrower who is using margin securities as collateral for a loan.

### Statutory Underwriter

*See* Involuntary (Statutory) Underwriter.

### Statutory Voting

A means by which a stockholder is given the right to cast one vote for each share owned in favor of or against each of a number of proposals or director/nominees at a formal meeting convened by the corporation.

### Stickering

Changing the official statement of a new issue by printing the altered information on adhesive-backed paper and "stickering" onto the statement.

### Sticky Deal

An underwriting that, for one reason or another, will be hard to market.

### Stock Ahead

An expression used on the floor of the New York Stock Exchange to signify that one or more brokers had made a prior bid (or offer) at the same price as an order you had entered. Sometimes a customer's order remains unexecuted for this reason. In other words, there is "stock ahead" of the order.

### Stock Clearing Corporation (SCC)

Formerly a NYSE subsidiary responsible for arranging daily transaction clearances, preparation of balance orders to receive and deliver, a single money settlement for members, and a centralized location for making physical deliveries of certificates. The Stock Clearing Corporation was merged into the National Securities Clearing Corporation.

### Stock Dividend Distribution

A distribution to shareholders made upon declaration by a corporation's board of directors. This distribution differs from the usual disbursement in that it is given in the form of additional shares of stock instead of money.

### Stockholder (Shareholder)

The owner of common or preferred stock.

### Stockholder of Record

Person named on the issuer's stock books as the owner.

### Stockholders' Equity

*See* Shareholders' (Stockholders') Equity.

### Stock List Department

A department of the NYSE responsible for (1) examining the eligibility of corporations applying for listing and trading on the exchange and (2) supervising distributions of proxies to beneficial owners of shares held in street name by member organizations.

### Stock Loan/Borrow

Brokerage firms constantly lend each other stock to cover short sales. The department in the firm that handles this activity is known as Stock Loan or Stock Loan/Borrow.

### Stock (or Bond) Power

A legal document, either on the back of registered stocks and bonds or attached to them, by which the owner assigns the interest in the corporation to a third party, allowing that party the right to substitute another name on the company records in place of the original owner's.

### Stock Record

The records of a brokerage firm showing the beneficial owner (long) and the location (short) of every security entrusted to the firm. Longs and shorts must be equal (in balance) since for every beneficial owner there must be a location.

### Stock Record Department

The department in a brokerage firm responsible for maintaining a balanced stock record.

### Stocks

Certificates representing ownership in a corporation and a claim on the firm's earnings and assets; they may yield dividends and can appreciate or decline in value.

*See* Authorized Stock; Common Stock; Issued-and-Outstanding Stock; Preferred Stock; Treasury Stock; Unissued Stock.

### Stock Watcher

A computerized service in the Stock Watch Department of the NYSE that keeps track of the trading activity and movements of listed stocks.

### Stop Limit Order

A memorandum that becomes a limit (as opposed to a market) order immediately after a transaction takes place at or through the indicated (memorandum) price.

### Stop Loss Order

A customer's order to set the sell price of a stock below the market price, thus locking in profits or preventing further losses.

### Stop Order

A memorandum that becomes a market order only if a transaction takes place at or through the price stated in the memorandum. Buy stop orders are placed above the market, and sell stop orders are placed below it. The sale that activates the memorandum is called the electing (activating or triggering) sale.

*See* Buy Stop Order; Market Order; Sell Stop Order.

### Stop-Out Price

The lower dollar price at auction for which Treasury bills are sold.

### Stopped Out

An expression reflecting a broker's unsuccessful attempt to improve upon the price of a transaction after having been guaranteed an execution price by the specialist.

### Stopping Stock

A specialist's guarantee of price to a broker, thus enabling the broker to try to improve upon that price without fear of missing the market.

### Straddle Option

One put and one call option on the same underlying security carrying the same striking price and expiration date.

### Straight-Line Depreciation

An accounting procedure for apportioning a corporation's cost of a qualified asset over its useful lifetime in equal increments.

### Strap Option

In the OTC market one put and two call options on the same underlying security carrying the same striking price and expiration date. The total premium for this quantity transaction is generally cheaper than if the options were purchased separately. This is an old term, not generally used.

### Strategy

A plan of selecting positions and executing transactions for the purpose of achieving the stated investment objectives.

### Street

"Wall Street"—that is, the New York financial community, as well as the exchanges throughout the country.

### Street Name

When securities have been bought on margin or when the customer wishes the security to be held by the broker/dealer, the securities are registered and held in the broker/dealer's own firm (or "street") name.

### Strike (Striking, Exercise) Price

The price at which an option may be exercised. That is, when the underlying stock reaches the strike price, an option holder may require the writer to perform the transaction as agreed upon in the original privilege.

### Striking Price Interval

A distance measured between striking prices on an underlying security. With some exceptions, the interval is normally 5 points for stocks selling up to $50 per share, 10 points for stocks between $50 and $200 per share, and 20 points for any stock thereafter.

### Strip Call

Reedeeming municipal bonds by calling some of each maturity.

### Strip Option

In the OTC market, one call and two put options on the same underlying security carrying the same striking price and expiration date. The total premium for this quantity transaction is generally cheaper than if the options were purchased separately. This is an old term, not generally used.

### Strip Order

An order to buy serial bonds in successive maturities.

### Subchapter S Corporation

A corporation that is not itself a taxable legal entity. Instead, it is taxed as a partnership.

### Subject Market (Price, Quote)

In the OTC market, a range of buying or selling prices quoted by market makers at which they are unable to trade immediately. Such prices are subject to verification by the parties whose market they represent.

### Subordinated Debt Instruments

A debt instrument requiring that repayment of principal may not be made until another debt instrument senior to it has been repaid in full.

### Subscription

An agreement to buy a new issue of securities. The agreement specified the *subscription price* (the price for shareholders before the securities are offered to the public). This right is called the *subscription privilege* or *subscription right.*

### Subscription Privilege (Preemptive Right)

A shareholder's right to purchase newly issued shares or bonds (before the public offering). It must be exercised within a fixed period, usually 30 to 60 days, before the privilege expires and becomes worthless.

### Subscription Ratio

The ratio of old stock to new stock offered as a subscription privilege.

### Subscription Right

A privilege granted to owners of certain stocks to purchase newly issued securities in proportion to their holdings, usually at values below the current market price. Rights have a market value of their own and are actively traded. They differ from warrants in that they must be exercised within a relatively short period of time.

### Subservicer

In the case of a mortgage pool, a lender subcontracted by a servicer to perform the ongoing services for the pool.

### Subsidiary

A company 50 percent of whose voting shares are owned by another company.

### Substantial Net Capital

Each member of the New York Stock Exchange is required to maintain "substantial net capital," as defined by NYSE Rule 325.

### Substantive Interest

A term referring to a matter raised at a corporate meeting that affects stockholder participation in the company. It includes a contest of control, changing the purpose of powers of the corporation, altering its capitalization, authorizing the expenditure of capital funds, and the like.

### Substitution (Swap)

The sale of one security in an account to use the proceeds to pay for the purchase of another security on the same trade date.

*See* Switch (Contingent or Swap) Order.

### Suitability

The appropriateness of a strategy or transaction, in light of an investor's financial means and investment objectives.

### Sum-of-Years' Digits Depreciation

A somewhat accelerated accounting procedure used to write off the cost of a qualified asset over the period of its useful lifetime.

### Summary Complaint Proceedings

In the event of a minor infraction of NASD Rules of Fair Practice, the Business Conduct Committee may offer the accused member a penalty of censure and/or fine up to $1,000 if the violator wishes to plead guilty and waive formal hearing and all rights of appeal.

### Sundry Asset

An item of value to be held by a corporation for an indefinite time. This category includes unimproved land and investments in subsidiary concerns.

### Sunshine Law

Law giving the public access to the meetings and records of government agencies (such as the SEC and the Commodities Futures Trading Commission).

### Super-Restricted Account

An old term no longer in use. A margin account in which the equity is less than 30% of the market value of the adjusted debit balance in the account.

### Support

In technical analysis, an area below the current price of the stock where the stock is in short supply and where the buyers are aggressive. The stock's price is likely not to go lower than this level, which is called a *support level.*

*See* Resistance.

### Support Level

*See* Support.

### Suspended Trading

The temporary ceasing of trading of an issue.

### Suspense Account

A record maintained by a broker/dealer to reflect unreconciled money and securities differences in its business activities.

### Synthetic Straddle

*See* Reverse Hedge.

### Swap

The agreement to exchange (or swap) one interest rate or currency for another between companies in two different countries.

Interest rate swaps usually exchange floating-rate payments for fixed-rate payments, although other types of swaps are done.

Currency swaps are agreements to deliver one currency against another at certain intervals.

### Swap Order/Transactions

*See* Switch (Contingent or Swap) Order.

### Sweetener

A special feature in a securities offering, such as convertibility, that encourages the purchase of the security.

### Switch (Contingent or Swap) Order

An order to buy one security and then sell another at a limit, or to sell one security and then to buy another at a limit. The transaction may also be called a proceeds sale if, as is usually the case, the proceeds of the sell order are applied against the expenses of the buy order.

### Syndicate

A group of investment bankers who purchase securities from the issuer and then reoffer them to the public at a fixed price. The syndicate is usually organized along historical or social lines, with one member acting as *syndicate manager*, who insures the successful offering of a corporation's securities.

### Synthetic Put

An unlisted security offered by some brokerage firms. The broker sells stock short and buys a call, giving the customer a "synthetic" put. Also known as a converted put.

### Synthetic Stock

An option strategy equivalent to the underlying stock where a long call and a short put become a synthetic long stock. A long put and a short call become a synthetic short stock.

### Tail

In a competitive underwriting, the decimals after a point bid.

In a U.S. Treasury auction, the difference between the average bid and the lowest competitive bid.

In reference to a Ginnie Mae, an amount added to the face value.

*See* Government National Mortgage Association.

### Tailgating

An account executive's purchase of a security for his/her own account right on the heels of a purchase of the same security for a customer.

### Take a Bath

Slang meaning to incur a large loss.

### Take a Flier

Slang meaning to enter into a highly speculative investment.

### Take a Position

To hold stocks or bonds, in either a long or short position.

To purchase securities as a long-term investment.

### Takedown

In a municipal underwriting, the price that syndicate members pay when they take bonds from the account.

In an underwriting, the number of securities that a syndicate member is supposed to sell.

### Take Off

The summary of daily changes in a security that is posted to the stock record.

### Take Out

The money that an investor "takes out" from an account when there is a net credit balance.

*See* Net Credit Balance.

### Take-Out Loan

The permanent financing that is provided following construction of a real estate project.

*See* Construction Loan.

### Takeover

The assumption of control over a corporation by another corporation, through acquisition or merger.

*See* Golden Parachute; Killer Bees; Poison Pill; Saturday Night Special; Shark Watcher; Tender Offer.

### Take Delivery

In commodities trading, the taking of physical delivery of a commodity under a futures or spot market contract.

In securities, accepting a receipt of stock or bond certificates after they have been purchased or transferred between accounts.

### TAN

*See* Tax Anticipation Note.

### Tape

A financial news service that reports the prices and sizes of transactions. Although this information was once reported on a paper tape from a "ticker tape" machine, it is now displayed on electronic screens. The name "tape," however, persists.

### Tape Racing

An account executive's executing personal orders before executing a sizable customer order, to take advantage of the large order's effect on prices.

### Tax Anticipation Bills (TAB)

Treasury bills with maturity dates fixed several days after a major tax payment date with a proviso enabling their holders to tender them at face value in satisfaction of their tax requirement and earn a little extra interest in the process.

### Tax Anticipation Note (TAN)

A short-term municipal note usually offered on a discount basis. The proceeds of a forthcoming tax collection are pledged to repay the note.

### Tax-Exempted Securities

Obligations issued by a state or municipality, or a state or local agency, whose interest payments (but not profits from purchase or sale) are exempted from federal taxation. The interest payment may be exempted from local taxation, too, if purchased by a resident of the issuing state. The term does not include U.S. government obligations.

*See* General Obligation (GO) Bond; Revenue Bonds.

### Tax-Sheltered Programs

A term used to describe investment programs that have only limited economic value compared with high risk but that are profitable from the standpoint of reducing federal income tax.

### Tax Straddle

Someone who has realized a short-term capital gain takes offsetting positions in commodity futures contracts so as to create a short-term loss, thereby reducing taxes on the net position in that year.

### Tax Swap

Selling a security at a loss, at the same time purchasing a similar security. The effect is to reduce tax liability.

### TBA

*See* To Be Announced.

### Technical Analysis

An approach to market theory stating that previous price movements, properly interpreted, can indicate future price patterns.

*See* Random Walk Theory.

### Technical Sign

A movement in a security's price that, under certain circumstances, indicates a short-term trend.

### Telephone Booths

Booths or cubicles ringing the stock exchange trading rooms that are used by member organizations to (1) receive orders from their offices, (2) distribute orders to brokers for execution, and (3) transmit details of the executed orders back to their offices.

### Temporary Specialist

An experienced member of the exchange appointed by a floor official to act as a specialist only in an emergency situation. His or her responsibilities are the same as those of a regular specialist.

*See* Associate Specialist; Relief Specialist.

### Tenants in Common

A form of joint ownership in which, upon the death of a tenant, the descendant's portion passes through probate instead of directly to the other tenants.

### Tenants by Entirety

A form of ownership by which assets legally transfer to the surviving spouse upon the death of either party in a marriage. If a securities account were so owned jointly by husband and wife, it would transfer to the surviving spouse upon the death of either tenant.

### Tender

To bid—to apply for purchase, as in government securities, at a price of the buyer's choosing.

### Tender Offer

A formal proposition to stockholders to sell their shares in response to a large purchase bid. The buyer customarily agrees to assume all costs and reserves the right to accept all, none, or a specific number of the shares presented for acceptance.

### 10K Report

A detailed report that corporations must file with the SEC.

### Tennessee Valley Authority (TVA)

A government-sponsored agency whose bonds are redeemable from the proceeds of the various power projects in the Tennessee River area. Interest payments on these bonds are fully taxable to investors.

### Ten Percent Guideline

Formula used in municipal debt issues analysis. The total bonded debt of a municipality shouldn't exceed 10 percent of the market value of the real estate within the municipality.

### Term Bond

A U.S. Treasury bond with a call privilege that becomes effective generally five years prior to maturity.

A large municipal bond issue with all the bonds maturing on the same date.

### Term Funds

Fed funds, when used in interbank transactions for terms of more than one day up to one year.

### Term Loan

Short-term debt with little or no amortization, so that the principal is paid in lump sum. These are typically secondary liens at high interest rates.

### Term REPO

A repurchase agreement whose life extends beyond the normal overnight agreement.

### Terms

The expiration date, striking price, and underlying stock of an option contract.

### Testamentary Trust

A legal instrument that appoints an individual or an institution to perform a specific function with a designated sum of money. The trust relationship becomes effective upon the death of its creator; its terms are spelled out in the descendant's will.

### The Market

A general term denoting the entire system for buying and selling securities.

### Theoretical Value

In the absence of actual market values, the value of stock offered under a preemptive privilege, which is determined by (1) subtracting the price of the new stock from the price of the old stock (cum rights) and (2) dividing the difference by the number of rights needed to subscribe to one new share plus one.

### Thin Market

*See* Narrow Market.

### Third Market

Transactions in exchange-listed stocks by OTC, nonmember broker/dealers of that exchange who specialize in such transactions.

### Third-Party Account

A brokerage account carried in the name of a person other than a customer. The practice is prohibited by NYSE regulation.

### Third-Party Check

A check drawn to the order of one person who endorses it to another person, who subsequently presents it to someone else in satisfaction of an obligation.

### Thirty-Day (Wash Sale) Rule

*See* Wash Sale Rule.

### Thirty-Day Visible Supply

Calendar published each Thursday by the *Daily Bond Buyer* listing new negotiated and competitive municipal securities that will come to market within the next 30 days.

### Three-Handed Deal

Colloquial expression for a municipal security issue underwriting consisting of serial maturities with two term maturities.

### Thrift Institutions

Savings banks, savings and loans, or credit unions. Also known as thrifts.

### Throwaway Offer

A nominal (approximate) bid or offer that should not be considered final.

### Tick

A transaction on the stock exchange.

*See* Minus Tick; Plus Tick; Zero-Minus Tick; Zero-Plus Tick.

### Ticker (Tape)

A trade-by-trade report in chronological order of trades executed, giving prices and volumes. Separate tapes exist for various markets. The mechanism used to be mechanical, but it is now some sort of electronic display.

### Tiered

When loans from several sources are obtained, the debt structure is said to be "tiered."

### Tight Market

An active, vigorous market with narrow bid-offer spreads.

### Tight Money

An economic condition characterized by scarce credit, generally the result of a money supply restricted by the Federal Reserve.

*See* Easy Money.

### TIGRs

*See* Treasury Investment Growth Receipts.

### Time Deposit

An account containing a currency balance pledged to remain at that bank for a specified, extended period in return for payment of interest.

### Time Spread

The term is used interchangeably with calendar spread.

### Time-Fixed Charges Earned

*See* Fixed Charge Coverage.

### Time Value

*See* Extrinsic Value.

### Time Value Premium

The amount an option's total premium exceeds its intrinsic value.

### Tip

A suggestion as to what to buy or sell that is based on "inside" information.

### To Be Announced (TBA)

Term applied to a security whose financial terms (issue date, maturity date, pool number, and so forth) are not yet available.

### Tokyo Stock Exchange

Second in size only to NYSE, the exchange is characterized by matched order clearance system and fixed, relatively high fees.

### Tombstone

The type of newspaper advertisement used for public offering. The ad simply and drably lists all the facts about the issue. Also called the offering circular.

### Top-Down Approach to Investing

An investment strategy in which an investor first determines the trends in the economy and then picks industries and companies benefiting from those trends.

### Total Capitalization

The aggregate value of a corporation's long-term debt, preferred, and common stock accounts—or, put another way, funded debt plus shareholders' equity.

### Total Cost

The contract price plus all expenses incurred on the purchase execution.

### Total Reserve

All the deposits that a bank has with the Federal Reserve plus all cash it has on hand.

### Total Return Concept

A strategy in covered call writing where the writer views the potential profit of the strategy as the sum of capital gains, dividends, and option premium income, rather than viewing each one of the three separately.

### Total Volume

A column in the listed stock and bond tables showing total shares of stocks traded (omitting the last two zeros) and the total par value of bonds traded (omitting the last three zeros).

### Trade Date

The date a trade was entered into, as opposed to settlement date.

### Trader

A person or firm engaged in the business of buying and selling securities, options, or commodities for a profit.

### Trade Registers

A summary, issued daily by the Clearing Corporation to each clearing member, itemizing by delivery month the previous net position and all the day's trades of the clearing member, with the pay or collect on each figured into the settlement price.

### Traders Ticket

In mortgage-backed trading, that expands the details of a trade from the trader's slate entry. A trader's ticket is completed only for broker/dealer trades.

### Trading Authorization

The legal right conferred by a person or institution upon another to effect the purchase and/or sale of securities in the former's account.

### Trading Crowd

Members of an exchange involved in the purchase and sale of a particular issue. They gather the specialist's position.

### Trading Floor

The location at any organized exchange where buyers and sellers meet to transact business.

### Trading Halts

Trading of index options may be halted when the current value of the underlying index is unavailable or when trading is halted in stocks accounting for more than a specified percentage of the value of the underlying index.

### Trading Post

Twenty-three locations on the floor of the NYSE that were 7-foot-high, horseshoe-shaped structures with an outside circumference of from 26 to 31 feet. The one exception is a table-like structure, Post 30, in the garage, where most inactive preferred stocks are traded in multiples of 10 shares. The posts have been replaced by a round structure with a lot of electronics display.

### Trading Rotation

The trading rotation is a system of opening the market on an options exchange. It is used to open trading in the morning and to reopen trading if a trading halt occurs during the day. Each option series is opened one at a time until all series in the same underlying stock have been given a chance to trade. After the rotation, simultaneous trading in all series then begins. Some exchanges use a closing rotation at the end of the day, which then officially closes the market.

### Trading to Total Volume (TTV)

The amount of trading in a security in which the specialist participates for his or her own account in relation to total volume in that security. The amount is computed by dividing the specialist's total dealings by twice the reported volume of shares.

### Trench (Tranch)

*See* Collateralized Mortgage Obligation.

### Transfer Agent

An agent of a corporation responsible for the registration of shareowners' names on the company records and the proper re-registration of new owners when a transfer of stock occurs.

### Transfer and Ship

Customer instructions to have securities transferred into his or her name and sent to his or her address.

### Treasury Bill

A federal bearer obligation issued in denominations of $10,000 to $1 million with a maturity date usually of three months to one year. It is fully marketable at a discount from face value (which determines the interest rate).

*See* Tax Anticipation Bill.

### Treasury Bill/Option Strategy

A method of investment where an investor uses approximately 90% of his or her funds in risk-free, interest-bearing assets, such as Treasury bills, while buying options with the remainder of the assets.

### Treasury Bond

A federal registered or bearer obligation issued in denominations of $500 to $1 million with maturities ranging from five to thirty-five years, carrying a fixed interest rate and issued, quoted, and traded as a percentage of its face value.

*See* Flower Bond; Term Bond.

### Treasury Note

A federal registered or bearer obligation issued in denominations of $1,000 to $500 million for maturities of one to ten years, carrying a fixed rate of interest. These notes are issued, quoted, and traded at a percentage of their face value.

### Treasury Securities

Debt obligations that the U.S. government issues and that the Treasury Department sells in the form of bills, notes, and bonds.

### Treasury Stock

Shares of stock required by a corporation through purchase, and occasionally by donation, which are treated as authorized-but-unissued stock for purposes of calculating dividend, voting, or earnings.

### Trend

Movement, up or down, in a security's market price, or in the market itself, for a period of six months or more.

### Trendline

The line superimposed by technical analysts on price plottings to indicate a price trend. Drawn beneath the prices, the line reflects an upward trend; above the prices, it means the trend is downward.

### Triangle

In technical analysis, a chart pattern of the stock price movements with the base at the left and the apex at the right. Also called a flag, coil, wedge, or pennant depending on the price movements.

### Triggering Sale

*See* Electing Sale.

### Triple Witching Hour

*See* Witching Hour.

### Trustee

Generally, a party (often a commercial bank) designated to supervise compliance with the terms of legal agreement. In the case of bonds, the trustee is designated by indenture.

### TTV

*See* Trading to Total Volume.

### Turkey

A security that is not doing an investor any good.

### TVA

*See* Tennessee Valley Authority.

### Twelve-Year Life

In mortgage-backed trading, the assumption that the cash flow from a mortgage will be level until the twelfth year, when the principal balance will be repaid in full.

### Twenty-Day (Cooling-Off) Period

A period of twenty calendar days following the filing of a registration statement with the SEC, during which (1) the SEC examines the statement for deficiencies; (2) the issuing corporation negotiates with an underwriting syndicate for a final agreement; and (3) the syndicate prepares for the successful distribution of the impending issue. The final day of the period is normally considered the effective date.

### Twenty-Five Percent Rule

In municipal securities analysis, a rule of thumb that an issuer's bonded debt should not exceed 25 percent of its annual budget.

### Twenty-Five Percent Cushion Rule

In the analysis of municipal revenue bonds, a rule of thumb that the revenue from the facility built with the bond issue's proceeds should exceed the cost of operations, maintenance, and debt service by 25 percent.

### Two-Dollar Broker

A member of the New York Stock Exchange who executes orders in any security for any organization, in return for which he receives a brokerage fee. Their fee, which is negotiable, is actually larger than $2 per trade. They are also known as independent brokers or agents.

### Type

A put is one type of option; a call is the other.

### U-4 Form

The form on which a securities firm sponsors an employee to take the Series 7 Registered Representative examination.

### Uncovered Option

*See* Naked Option.

### Uncovering an Option

The act of selling a position (or covering a short position) that had been used in conjunction with a covered option, thereby leaving the option uncovered.

### Underlying Security

The security that an investor has the right to buy or sell according to the terms of a listed option contract.

### Undervalued

A term used to describe a security that is trading at a lower price than it should.

*See* Overvalued; Fair Value.

### Underwriter

Also known as an "investment banker" or "distributor," a middleman between an issuing corporation and the public. The underwriter usually forms an underwriting group, called a syndicate, to limit risk and commitment of capital. He or she may also contract with selling groups to help distribute the issue—for a concession. In the distribution of mutual funds, the underwriter may also be known as a "sponsor," "distributor," or even "wholesaler." Investment bankers also offer other services, such as advice and counsel on the raising and investment of capital.

### Underwriter's Retention

The percentage of total issue to which each member of an underwriter's group is entitled and which he or she distributes to customers. The retained amount is usually equal to about 75 percent of the member's total financial commitment. The syndicate manager decides, on behalf of the other members, how to distribute the rest of the issue (or "the pot"), and how it is to be sold to institutional investors (group sales) or reserved for handling by selling groups.

*See* Philadelphia Plan; Western Account.

### Underwriting Agreement

The contract between the investment banker and the corporation, containing the final terms and prices of the issue. It is signed either on the evening before or early in the morning of the public offering date (effective date).

### Underwriting Compensation (Spread)

The gross profit realized by an underwriter equal to the difference between the price he paid to the issuing corporation and the price of the public offering.

### Undivided Account

In an underwriting agreement, an arrangement for the sharing of liability in which each member of the syndicate is liable for any unsold portion of an issue. The degree of liability is based on each member's percentage distribution.

*See* Syndicate.

### Uniform Commercial Code

A national statute standardizing commercial practice.

### Uniform Gifts to Minors Act

A simplified law that enables minors to own property or securities in a beneficial fashion without need of trust instruments or other legal documents. In the securities industry, the term describes securities bought and sold under the provisions of this law that allows someone of legal age to serve as custodian for the minor's assets.

### Uniform Practice Code ("the Code")

A code established and maintained by the NASD Board of Governors that regulates the mechanics of executing and completing securities transactions in the OTC market.

### Uniform Practice Committee

An NASD district subcommittee that disseminates information and interpretations handed down by the Board of Governors regarding the Uniform Practice Code.

### Unincorporated Association

A group of people and/or institutions existing without the benefit of incorporating. Included in this category are partnerships and, in certain cases, churches, schools, and charitable organizations.

### Unissued Stock

That portion of authorized stock not distributed among investors.

### Unit Investment Trust Company

An investment company (1) organized under a trust indenture rather than a corporate charter; (2) directed by a body of trustees rather than a board of directors; and (3) able to issue only redeemable shares of beneficial interest to represent an undivided participation in a unit of specified securities.

*See* Fixed Trust; Participating Trust.

### United Account

*See* Severally and Jointly.

### United States Government Securities

Debt issues of the U.S. government (Treasury Department), backed by the government's unlimited power of taxation, such as Treasury bills, notes, bonds, and Series EE and Series HH bonds.

*See* Marketable Securities; Nonmarketable Securities.

### Unlisted Security

A security that is not traded on an exchange. Usually called an over-the-counter security.

### Unmatched Trade

A trade in which both sides (trader and customer) do not agree on the details.

### Unqualified Legal (Clean) Opinion

An unconditional affirmation of a security's legality, rendered either before or after the security is sold.

*See* Qualified Legal Opinion.

### Unrealized Profit and Loss

The profit and loss for each trade before settlement.

### Unsecured Obligation (Bond)

A debt instrument whose repayment is backed solely by the creditworthiness of the issuer. No specific property is pledged as security. Also called a "debenture."

### Unwind a Trade

To undo a transaction, such as "unwinding" a short sale with a purchase.

To correct an erroneous transaction.

### Up and Out Option

A block of at least ten put options with the same striking price and expiration date carrying a provision for immediate cancellation of the exercise privilege if the underlying stock rises by a predetermined, agreed-upon amount in the marketplace.

### Up Delta

*See* Delta.

### Upgrade

Raising a security's rating by improving the credit quality of the issuer or issuers.

### Uptick

*See* Plus-Tick.

### Uptrend

Any generally upward movement in a security's price.

### Variable Annuity Contract Plan

An investment contract prepared by a life insurance company designed to offer continuous income through participation in a mutual fund portfolio; some life insurance is included as a death benefit and as an additional attraction.

### Variable Rate

Interest rate on a security that is subject to change, commonly in connection with the rates paid on selected issues of Treasury securities. Also called floating rate.

### Variable Rate Mortgage

*See* Adjustable Rate Mortgage.

### Variable Ratio Hedging

A system of taking long and/or short positions in different securities and/or options for the purpose of creating a hedged position using other than a one-for-one relationship between the positions.

*Example:* Buy 2 IBM Jan 260 Calls, Sell 5 IBM Jan 280 Calls.

### Variable Ratio Write

In options writing, a strategy in which an investor owns 100 shares of the underlying security and writes two call options against it with each option having a different striking price.

### Vault Cash

All the cash in a bank's vault.

### Velocity (of Money)

The number of times a dollar changes hands in one year. Given a fixed money supply, increased velocity is usually a sign to the Federal Reserve that an increase in the money supply is needed.

### Venture Capital Company

An investment company whose objective is to invest in new or underdeveloped companies.

### Vertical Line Charting

A method of technical analysis in which the high and low for the period (usually a day) are shown as a vertical line on the chart, with the closing price shown as a small horizontal line.

### Vertical Spread

The simultaneous purchase and sale of options of the same class having the same expiration date but different striking prices. Also known as a price spread.

### Veterans Administration (VA)

An independent federal agency created in 1944 to administer benefit programs that would help returning veterans adjust to civilian life. The VA home loan guaranty program encourages long-term, low-down-payment mortgages to eligible veterans by guaranteeing the lenders against loss. The VA also guarantees mobile home loans to eligible veterans.

### Visible Supply

*See* Thirty-Day Visible Supply.

### Volatility

A measurement of the price movement of a security during a specific period.

### Volume

Number of bonds or shares traded during specific periods, such as daily, weekly, or monthly.

### Volume Deleted

A ticker tape announcement to signify that quantities of less than 5,000 shares per transaction will not appear until the ticker tape can stay abreast of trading activity on the stock exchange floor. It appears when the tape falls two minutes behind.

### Volume Resumed

The volume-deleted condition is no longer in effect.

### Voluntary Accumulation Plan

An informal mutual fund investment program allowing customers to arrange purchases in the frequency and numbers of dollars at their own choosing yet providing them with benefits normally available only to larger investors. Sales charge percentage requirements are constant throughout the life of the plan and are therefore "level-loaded."

### Voluntary Association

A form of business dating back to medieval England, involving a partnership with continuing existence but unlimited financial liability. The NYSE was originally a voluntary association.

### Voluntary Underwriter

An individual or corporation that purchases a security from an issuer or affiliated person and offers it for public sale under an effective registration statement.

### Voting Trust

The deposit of shares by shareholders with a commercial bank (trustee) for the purpose of gaining long-term corporate control.

### Voting Trust Certificate (VTC)

A certificate issued by a commercial bank in exchange for common stock deposited under terms of a voting trust. These certificates are comparable to the common stock itself but do not carry voting privileges in the affairs of the underlying corporation.

### VTC

*See* Voting Trust Certificate.

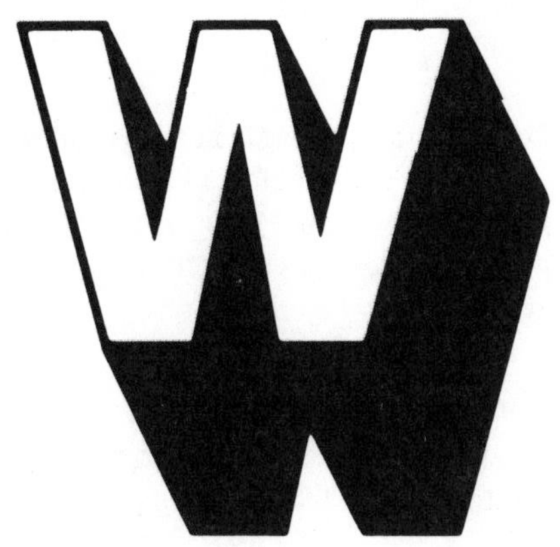

### Wallflower

A stock that investors are, by and large, just not attracted to.

### War Babies

Securities of corporations engaged in defense contracts. Also known as war brides.

### Warehousing

The illegal sale of a corporate security with a provision for its repurchase by the seller at some future date and at a prearranged price.

### Warrant

An inducement attached to new securities in distribution giving purchasers a long-term (usually a five- to ten-year) privilege of subscribing to one or more shares of stock reserved for them by the corporation from its unissued or treasury stock reserve.

*See* Subscription Right.

### Wash Sale

For regulatory purposes, the purchase and sale of the same security at the same time and price without any real change of ownership. This practice is outlawed under Section 10 of the Securities Exchange Act of 1934.

For tax purposes a sale at a loss and repurchase of the same or a similar issue, within thirty days before or after the first transaction, while intending to use that loss to offset capital gains or taxable income in that year. The loss is generally not allowed as a tax deduction under the 1954 Tax Code.

*See* Manipulation.

### Watch List

A list of securities, established by a broker/dealer or an exchange, that are under scrutiny for evidence of illegal or unethical practices.

### Watered Stock

A corporation's issuance of additional shares without increasing its capital. Also called diluting the shares.

### WD

*See* When Distributed.

### Weak Market

A market characterized by a greater number of sellers than buyers, which creates a general downtrend in prices.

### Wedge

*See* Triangle.

### Western Account

An agreement among underwriters regarding liability, in which each member of the syndicate is liable only for the amount of its participation in, but not for the unsold portion of, the issue.

*See* Severally but Not Jointly; Syndicate.

### W Formation

*See* Double Bottom.

### When Issued/When Distributed Contract

A delivery contract involving securities (stocks or bonds) that have been proposed for distribution but not yet issued. The date of delivery is set for some time in the future by the NASD Uniform Practice Committee or the appropriate stock exchange, as the case may be.

### White Knight

Colloquial expression for a person or firm who blocks a hostile takeover attempt by taking over the target company itself.

### Whole Loan

A pool of mortgages that are sold to a dealer in their entirety.

### Wholesaler

*See* Underwriter.

### Whoops

Securities of the Washington Public Power Supply System (WPPS).

### WI

*See* When Issued.

### Widget

A fictitious manufactured product used in textbook examples, especially accounting problems.

Slang for the plastic holder delivered through a pneumatic tube.

### Window Settlement

Transactions that are not cleared through the SCC or NCC and that are completed in the office of the purchasing firm by means of certificate delivery versus immediate payment.

### Wire House

Any large exchange member firm.

### Wire Room

An area in each branch office and in the home office where messages may be received and sent using machinery that creates a printed copy of the messages. Message traffic normally consists of order data, reports of order executions, trade settlement information, and other sales data.

### Witching Hour

Program trading, usually conducted by major Wall Street firms for their own trading accounts, involves the purchase or sale of huge blocks of stocks, set off against large positions in the options and futures markets in order to profit from changes in their relationships to each other.

Such trading, which did not exist before 1982, has created last-minute chaos on the New York Stock Exchange on "triple-witching-hour" days when the options and futures contracts expire all at once.

"Triple witching" occurs four times a year, on the third Friday of the last month of each quarter.

The action will be watched all the more carefully because Federal regulators have recently expressed concerns about the volatility that has resulted from program trading.

### With-or-Without a Sale Order (WOW)

An odd-lot limit order to buy or sell either at a price derived from an effective round lot quotation (with a sale) or at the existing round lot quotation plus differential (without a sale), whichever occurs first in accordance with the customer's limit.

### Withholding

A failure by a broker/dealer to make a bona fide distribution of a hot issue, thus encouraging demand at a premium price. This practice is a violation of the NASD Rules of Fair Practice.

*See* Free-Riding.

### Without Dividend

*See* Ex-Dividend.

### Wooden Ticket

Confirming execution of a customer's order without actually executing it.

### Working Capital

*See* Net Working Capital.

### Working Capital Acceptance

Used by banks to finance unsecured loans, chiefly during periods of tight money. The acceptance reflects a time draft drawn by the borrower at the time the loan is established. The time draft, which will repay the loan when it comes due, is then stamped "accepted by the bank." This creates a marketable instrument now carrying the backing of the bank, which the bank can sell in the open market. Working capital BAs are not eligible for discount at the Fed.

### Working Capital Ratio

*See* Current Ratio.

### Workout Market

In the OTC market, a range of prices quoted by a market maker who is not certain that a market is available, but who feels he or she can "work one out" within a reasonable period of time.

### World Bank

Another name for the International Bank for Reconstruction and Development.

### WOW Order

*See* With-or-Without a Sale Order (WOW).

### Wraparound Mortgage

A secondary lien against property that incorporates the balance owed under a prior lien in the face value of the debt. When payment of principal and interest is received, the holder of the wraparound mortgage pays the mortgagee of the prior lien.

### Wrinkle

Colloquial term for a feature in a security that could benefit the holder.

### Write

The process of selling an option. The writer is the investor who sells the option.

### Write-Out

An exchange floor procedure by which specialists are allowed to buy stock for themselves from a customer's offering in their books, or sell from their accounts to a customer's bid. They must, however, allow the broker who entered the order to execute and "write out" the confirmation of the transaction and earn the contingent brokerage fee.

### Writer

*See* Option Writer.

An insurance underwriter.

### X

*See* Ex-Dividend (Without Dividend) Date.

### XCH

*See* Ex-Clearing House.

### XD

Shorthand notation meaning "ex-dividend."

*See* Ex-Dividend (Without Dividend) Date.

### X Dis

*See* Ex-Distribution.

### XRT

*See* Ex-Rights.

### XW

*See* Ex-Warrants.

### Yankee Bond

A dollar-denominated, foreign-issued bond that is registered for sale in the U.S.

### Yankee CD

A dollar-denominated, foreign-issued time deposit that is registered for sale in the U.S.

### Yellow Sheets

A daily publication of the National Quotation Bureau giving markets in corporate debt securities.

*See* Pink Sheets.

### Yield (Rate of Return)

The percentage return on an investor's money in terms of current prices. It is the annual dividend/interest per share or bond, divided by the current market price of that security.

### Yield Curve

Graph depicting the relation of interest rates to time: time is plotted on the *x*-axis, and yields on the *y*-axis. The curve shows whether short-term interest rates are higher or lower than long-term rates. A *positive yield curve* results if short-term rates are lower, and a *negative yield curve* results if short-term rates are higher. A *flat yield curve* results if long- and short-term rates do not differ greatly. Generally, the yield curve is positive because investors tie up their money for longer periods and are rewarded with better yields.

### Yield to Average Life

A bond's yield to maturity when its maturity is equal to the average life of a corresponding pass-through.

### Yield to Half Life

Yield to the point at which half of the original principal is paid.

### Yield to Maturity

The calculation of an average rate of return on a bond (with a maturity over one year) if it is held to its maturity date and if all cash flows are reinvested at the same rate of interest. It includes an adjustment for any premium paid or discount received. It is a calculation used to compare relative values of bonds.

### Yo-Yo Stock

A stock whose price rises and drops often and quickly.

### Zero-Coupon CMOs

CMO bonds that are either true zero coupon instruments or accrual bonds. An accrual (or compound interest) bond is a coupon bond that, during part of its life, accumulates accrued interest as increased principal rather than as cash paid. This accumulation is called "accretion."

### Zero-Coupon Discount Security

A debt security that offers no payments of interest—only payment of full face value at maturity— but that is at a deep discount from face value.

### Zero-Minus Tick

A transaction of the exchange at a price equal to that of the preceding transaction but lower than the last different price.

### Zero-Plus Tick

A transaction on the exchange at a price equal to that of the preceding transaction but higher than the last different price.